I'M NOT A
QUITTER
REBELIOUS HOPE

Ray of Sunshine

RAYMOND A COOKE

I'm Not a Quitter - Rebelious Hope
Copyright © 2021 by Raymond A Cooke

All rights reserved. No part of this publication may be reproduced, distributed, or transmitted in any form or by any means, including photocopying, recording, or other electronic or mechanical methods, without the prior written permission of the author, except in the case of brief quotations embodied in critical reviews and certain other non-commercial uses permitted by copyright law.

Tellwell Talent
www.tellwell.ca

ISBN
978-0-6452634-2-8 (Hardcover)
978-0-6452634-0-4 (Paperback)
978-0-6452634-3-5 (eBook)

DEDICATION

Dedicated to my siblings; my two children, Ingrid Geraldine Cooke and her family, Graydon Steven Cooke and his family; their mother my late wife, Theresa Philomena Cooke; and my present wife, for the last 31 years, Annie Evelyn Cooke. Finally, my 6 grandchildren: Dylon, Jye, Aiden, Cooper, Lily and Xavier. Above all I wish to extend my sincere thanks to my dear wife Evelyn, for her proofreading and spending many hours going over my typing, manuscript and supporting me along this journey, that I had embarked on in the late stages of my life.

TABLE OF CONTENTS

Introduction vii

Chapter 1	Dr Graham's Homes, Kalimpong, India...................	1
Chapter 2	Cottage life	7
Chapter 3	Life in Dr Graham's Homes	14
Chapter 4	St Thomas Boys' School days - Kolkata 1960-1963	25
Chapter 5	Meeting my parents for the first time	28
Chapter 6	My life and work in Calcutta	35
Chapter 7	Meeting my first wife Theresa....................................	38
Chapter 8	Leaving India for a new life in Australia	42
Chapter 9	Arrival and work experience in Australia	48
Chapter 10	Arrival of Theresa from India and our marriage	51
Chapter 11	My RAAF Career Begins...	58
Chapter 12	A family in crisis	78
Chapter 13	My RAAF comrades' gift of friendship.....................	83
Chapter 14	Our worst fear...	88
Chapter 15	A medical dairy in chronological order of Theresa Philomena Cooke..	91
Chapter 16	A new chapter in my life...	100
Chapter 17	The turnaround of my life in an upward direction	105
Chapter 18	Our special friends Edward and Jeba Martin for the last 31 years...	112
Chapter 19	Moving into our retirement home 5 May 2005..........	120
Chapter 20	Visit to my first home Dr Graham's Homes, Kalimpong, WB India 12-17 October 2012.......................	127
Chapter 21	The travel bug after marriage to Evelyn 1990-2019	133
Chapter 22	2019-2021 the coronavirus strikes the world COVID-19 pandemic	135

INTRODUCTION

The title of this book came to me when I saw this beautiful lady dying of cancer called "Nightbird "on *AGT* (*America's Got Talent*). Her actual name is Jane. She was with Christopher Cuomo on the CNN *Cuomo Primetime* show on 4 July 2021. It was a beautiful story of hope, courage, love and above all inspiration.

I wish to share my story in the hope that it will inspire and give solace and comfort to those who are going through difficult paths in their respective lives. I do believe through my personal experience in life, through health issues, tragedy and heartache, there is always hope and a bright light at the end of that dark tunnel. As one of our Prime Ministers Malcolm Frazer once said, "Life was not meant to be easy".

Ruth Cummings (Smith) was a nurse and missionary in India in the 1960s and for a further 10 years, and she was the first person that I had ever felt as a mother image for me. She bestowed love towards me, during the most difficult time of my young life. On 14 August 1960, I had a severe asthma attack and was carried up to the hospital in Dr Graham's Homes by a sturdy friend George Borthwick, for the last few hundred yards up the stone steps, past the chapel. I was greeted by Sister Ruth Cummings (Smith) who took me in and reassured me that all would be well. That night after Dr Rao visited me and tried to stabilize my condition, I went into a coma and did not wake till 20 August 1960. It was the first time I had experienced pure love and dedication. Ruth had stayed by my side during the whole episode. I speak to her on a regular basis even to this day. She tells me that she did it for Jesus. I will never forget her gift of love and sacrifice for me.

I had never known love in a way that a parent does, as I did not have anyone, and this is one of the reasons I cannot express emotion or love on the level that a father or mother should, as I did not know or experience that love or commitment from a parent. Even when I eventually had my own children, it was something I had to learn from scratch.

This story has many parts, prior to my birth in a troublesome time for the world in 1945. My father was born in 1918 at the conclusion of World War II. In 1919 my mother was born, as the Spanish flu pandemic was causing further havoc, death and destruction of life as we know it today. I am proud to have been born in India, and though known as an Anglo-Indian, I always felt a deep love for the country of my birth and made it a point to keep up the language skills I learned growing up. I feel very comfortable speaking in Hindi, even though my mother tongue was English. As I grew up in India, I will always cherish the food, tastes, smells, poverty, rich culture, the assortment of languages and dialects that are spoken in each state in India, and the good and the bad, and day-to-day memories of life in Calcutta, India.

Though I have lived two-thirds of my life in Australia, I still feel the affinity and love of the country of my birth. I am passionate and even to this day, even though I have lived and raised a family in Australia for over 50 years, I still always object or get passionate when we are put into categories of us and them. We need to coexist in this world of all races, religions, cultures and ethnic background. Colour of skin is only skin deep. We all bleed the same colour of red that runs through our veins. I love India as that is where my roots are. One of my strengths and weakness is my love for India. One can call it patriotism or nationalism. In my case I love both Australia and India. However, one should be careful about the danger of extreme nationalism. Once when my closest friend (he is also of Indian origin) joked to fellow cruise members that "Ray is Pakistani" I was very upset. This incident could have damaged our valuable relationship and friendship. I realise that extreme nationalism may bring not only conflict, but tension, misunderstanding and war among nations.

The advancement of DNA science has enabled me to find my family roots on my mother's side. The records I found using DNA go back a long way. My grandmother on my mother's side was one of four children: Lionel, Vera, Gladys and Albert.

I do not know very much about my early childhood. I know for a fact I was born on Saturday 29 December 1945 at home in Wellesley St,

Calcutta, Bengal, India. Probably with the help of a local midwife, as was the practice at the time, especially if you were poor and could not afford to go to hospital at the very end of a tumultuous year. I was baptised in St Thomas Catholic Church, Middleton Row, Calcutta WB India, early in the new year 1946. My 3 older brothers, Donovan, Winston and Errol also attended Dr Graham's Homes. It was much later I was able to find out, to my surprise, that on the death of my grandfather both my mother and her sister Alice attended Dr Graham's Homes, from April 1926 through their conclusion of their schooling. My mother never mentioned that to me. When I did go to my old school in October 2012, I was given access to the records held in the school office. It was such an eye opener. I was given to believe I was an orphan, and had accepted my fate, but those were the good old days, where much was swept under the carpet. I was able to view the records of my mother and her sister Alice and see the dates we were all admitted to Dr Graham's Homes.

I was number 6 of 12 children, two older brothers Victor and Gordon died when they were babies of malnutrition, and my younger sister Judy Susan Cooke was born on 13 November 1949. She did attend Dr. Graham's Homes in Elliott Cottage and left school in 1962. We were not even advised of her arrival in the school. She is now widowed and lives with her 4 boys in Hyderabad.

Little did I know that five of my younger siblings would be given up for adoption over the years, as my parents could not look after them. There were one boy and four girls. Gloria Cooke (dob approx. 1966 and whereabouts unknown) went with her adopted parents to England. Vernon Wilson (dob 17 June 1958) and Marcella Wilson (Barnes) (dob 20 November 1962 – was then a baby) were both adopted together to a family and went to England. Rosalind (31 July1958) was adopted to a family who migrated to Canada.

Rosalind lives in Toronto with her husband and three boys. Rosalind came to visit us in Australia in 2000 (after 43 years) and met our mum and her four brothers Donavan, Winston (deceased 06 December 2002), Errol and I who reside in Australia. There was so much to catch up on after all those years. We met her 3 boys in the years later.

Serina was adopted to a family and lives in Bombay. She has two girls and a boy (not much know of). My brother Errol and I had assisted financially in her daughters' Sharon and Evelyn's education. Sharon became a schoolteacher, married and had a son. Tragically she passed away early this year (2021) leaving behind her 6-year-old son and her husband. Evelyn is married and lives in Chennai

My brother Vernon did come out to Australia, after my older brother Errol found him and our sister Marcella, who tragically was killed in a hit and run accident on 19 February 2008, while on her way to work. I had spoken to her on the phone, when mum was still alive. Quite to my surprise she sounded so much like our mother. Both she and Vernon were planning to come to Australia to meet the families, but Marcella was unfortunately killed even before she could meet the families. By the time Vernon arrived in Australia, our mother had died, and he missed meeting her by a couple of months. It was ironic that Vernon's visit coincided with the collection of her ashes. I asked him if he would like to come and place the urn with her ashes in the Remembrance Wall, to which he agreed. We did that together, just Vernon, my elder brother Errol and I.

When my wife and I visited India, we made a point to try and catch up with my two sisters, Judy and Serina. We were able to catch up with Judy and her family but not Serina, as she could not be located. But we did catch up with her daughter Sharon. We arrived in Mumbai on 09 October 2012, and Sharon, my niece (she was single then) came to meet us at a restaurant. It just happened to be her 27th birthday. That again was a very emotional meeting and we had so much news to catch up on. She was so happy as we celebrated her 27th birthday and organised for the band to sing the "Happy Birthday" song and to cut a cake for her.

We left for Calcutta (Kolkata) to find my birthplace and places that I had lived and worked in. This was a wonderful experience after spending almost 45 years in Australia, to come back to all the nostalgic places in my life.

The above events in history help to show my connection to historic events, from the birth of my parents to my own birth on Saturday 29 December 1945 in Wellesley Street Calcutta, Bengal India, the fourth day after Christmas and two days before the new year of 1946, through records cited and obtained from Dr Graham's Homes, Kalimpong, West Bengal, India.

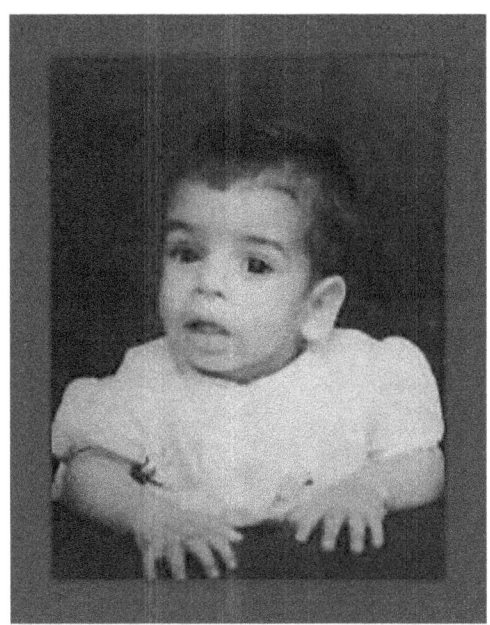

The first picture of the author -1947.

The 3 Cooke brothers, Raymond Errol & Winston at the back – 1953.

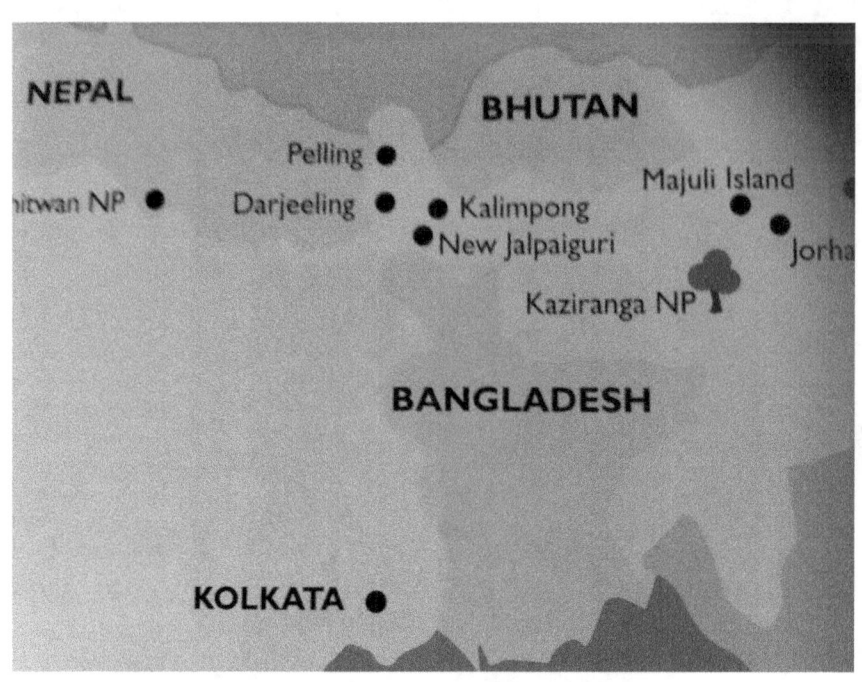

Location map of Kalimpong in WB INDIA

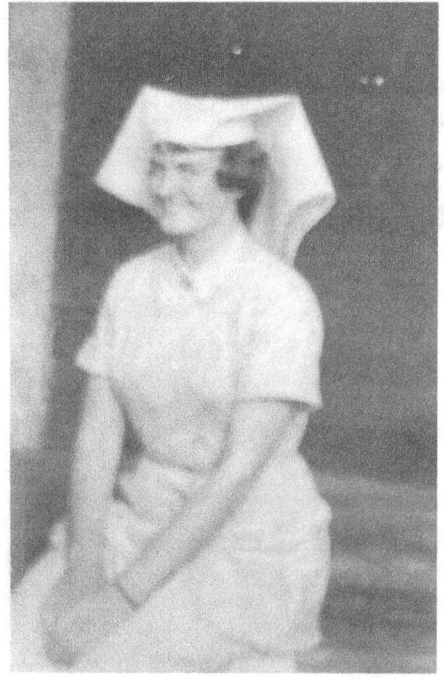

Sister Ruth Cummings (Smith) DGH – 1960.

My sister Rosalind and her biological mother after nearly 45 years separation in Australia January 2000.

Rosalind reunites with her mother & 4 brothers (Raymond, Errol, Winston & Don) in Australia after 40 plus years with her 4 older brothers. January 2000.

My sister Rosalind with 3 boys Jeffey, Marcus & Andrew.

My sister Rosalind meets my other family, my wife's side L-R Ester & Barry Gracie, Evelyn, Rosalind, Rajina and Brother Ray of Sunshine standing 2000.

Rosalind reunites with her 2 sisters Judy, and her 3 boys & Serna with her 2 girls Sharon & Evelyn standing in the front row in 7.18.1919.

Brother Vernon and Sister Marcela in Woolverhampton – UK.

Brother Vernon and Sister Marcella, as teenagers in the UK.

Brothers Errol and Raymond – OGB reunion 22.09.2011.

The 5 brothers reunite after 46 years (L-R Winston, Vernon, Raymond, Donovan & Errol) – Christmas 2001.

CHAPTER 1

Dr Graham's Homes, Kalimpong, India

Dr Rev John Anderson Graham was born in London 08 September 1861. His wife Katherine Graham was born 14 December 1861. They married on 15 January 1889 two days after he was ordained on 13 January 1889, and five days before he gave his final sermon in Scotland on 20 January 1889.

He arrived in Calcutta (Kolkata) on 21 March 1889. He came out to India as a Scottish missionary in 1889. After nearly 8 weeks travelling from Scotland via Switzerland, he arrived in Calcutta (Kolkata) on 21 March 1889. He preached his first sermon in India in Scots Kirk, Dalhousie Square, Calcutta the next day and then proceeded to Darjeeling. After one night's stop the party proceeded by ponies till, they arrived in Kalimpong. Dr Graham was a visionary who saw the need of the local people working in the tea gardens of Darjeeling and the district situated just south of the then Kingdom of Sikkim and between Nepal and the Kingdom of Bhutan.

Dr Graham founded the original St Andrews Colonial Homes on 24 September 1900, with six impoverished Anglo-Indian children of mixed race from the tea gardens in Assam. He and his wife had both learned to speak Nepalese and Hindi and his vision was to one day have 600 children. He based the planning of the Homes on a down-to-earth approach and was required to translate this dream into a reality. The planning was greatly influenced by the work of William Quarrier and by the homes he had established at The Bridge of Wier in West Scotland. He had built cottages on a large estate, and in each cottage were houseparents, who acted as substitute parents who looked after the needs and wants of the children from the Glasgow slums. His idea was to remove the children to the country away from their grim and harsh surroundings, and with houseparents carefully selected for their Christian commitment to look after them and be concerned about their general welfare. Dr Graham had seen the Quarrier Homes when on leave in Scotland and liked what he saw. With this example in mind, this was the kind of home that he envisioned for Kalimpong in India. It was not to be a Victorian-style orphanage, which was austere, loveless and forbidding. The vision of his children's home of the Himalayas was to be a home of flowers, fresh air and sunshine, but above all a place where the children could find a place for themselves and call home.

Dr Graham had boundless faith that the work he was doing was God's work. He discovered two basic reasons for his plan to work: firstly, that for the nature of the work he was trying to accomplish, he was assured of government support. At the time, government officials were happy that a private person was willing to take on this delicate and awkward role.

Government officials from viceroy to governors of states offered their wholehearted support during the initial stages of the growth of the Homes and were instrumental in their success. The help and encouragement by many influential people were seen as an asset to his cause.

The second reason was the growth of the British population, and there was great wealth among them at that time in India. The industrial revolution had come to India and fortunes were to be made by tea, jute, engineering and other modern industries. The British were able to retire at the age of 50 and had made enough money to live in luxury for the rest of their lives. They amassed their wealth and began to pour out of India. Dr Graham was a humble man and had no compunction of doing the rounds of large companies with his begging bowl. The tea companies were one of his obvious targets. Dr Graham formed a very influential board of management in India with Lieutenant Governor of Bengal Sir John Woodburn as the honorary president, the chief secretary of government as the president of the board, and a local tea planter as the chairman of the executive committee. The other members of the board of management were representatives of high government officials, tea planters, missionaries and businessmen of Calcutta (Kolkata) and Darjeeling merchants. This board was high-powered government department heads and members who were influential in their respective fields of business. Rev John Anderson Graham received his doctorate in divinity from his old university in Edinburgh, Scotland in 1904. On 28 May 1931, Dr Graham was appointed as the moderator of the Church of Scotland in India. Dr Graham was ably assisted by Mr James Purdy, as his right hand many for many years. The Katherine Memorial Chapel was opened on 24 December 1925. The chapel was built with labour and stonework from the local area, built to honour Dr Graham's wife. She passed away on 15 May 1919, which devastated Dr Graham, as she had been with him all their married life. Her work in Kalimpong for the women of the district included teaching them a craft and building the Arts and Craft Centre. She was also the cottage superintendent of the homes.

The Katherine Memorial Chapel was built with donations from all over India and overseas, at a cost of Rs200,000 (200,000 rupees) or at the time 12,000 British pounds. Dr Douglas Strachan was one of the greatest artists of his time, responsible for the revival of stained-glass work in Scotland. He charged half the cost for the construction of the three stained-glass windows. Two of the windows were donated by former pupils of the school, and the third was donated by the artist himself. This chapel was built as a fitting legacy of Katherine's dedication and work for Dr Graham's Homes.

Dr and Mrs Graham -1918.

Mr James Purdy and Dr Graham.

Dr Graham, The school and Mt Kangchenjunga.

Dr Graham's Homes Kalimpong India with
The Katherine memorial chapel.

Dr. and Mrs. Graham buried in the School Cemetery.

CHAPTER 2

Cottage life

Over the years 1900-1930 the government was extremely supportive and gave Dr Graham grants of Rs3,000 toward the construction of the first home at Rs3,750 Woodburn and further grants of Rs5 per child each month. This practical and financial assistance continued for many years. The first cottage was opened on 04 November 1901 and was called Woodburn Cottage, named after none other than Lt Governor Sir John Woodburn, who opened it in person followed by the laying of the foundation stone for the second cottage Elliot named after his predecessor, who happened to be the deputy lieutenant governor. Anecdotally, this double ceremony became the norm: as one cottage opened another foundation stone was laid and this is how Dr Grahams Homes (DGH) became the place we OGBs (Old Girls & Boys) have called home for the last 120 years.

Many other cottages, teachers' residences, guest houses and holiday homes were constructed, such as Ahava and James Purdie House, named after Mr James Purdy, who was Dr Graham's righthand man for many years, who lived to the age of 90. There were six girls' cottages: the two listed above followed Woodburn, Elliott, McGregor (1912), Mansfield, Bene, Birissa (the name derived from the donations by business leaders in the provinces of Bihar and Orrisa, adjacent to the state of Bengal). There were eight boys' cottages, Scottish Canadian (1912) Heathland (1914), Assam, Hart (1916), Laidlaw, Edinburgh (1915) and Wiston (1921), Calcutta and Assam. Then there were two hostels, Frazer and Willingdon (1935), built to cater for the elder boys, some of whom were undergoing agricultural training on the farm. It was a fully functioning farm, with a herd of cows, imported Angus bulls and a piggery, and a chicken pen and fish hatchery that were built over the years. This was where we got all our fresh meat, poultry, eggs, fish, fresh milk and all the different fruit in season like peaches, bananas, plumbs, mulberries, guavas and of course many varieties of mangoes. There was also an assortment of all kinds of vegetables. There were other buildings such as Christianson Farm Steading and Central Providence Farmhouse and Lucia King for infants and toddlers. The Main School Building with Jarvie Hall was there to conduct assemblies, movie nights and concerts, had a classroom block for primary students, a classroom block for senior students, the principal's office and the science block. Its McRoberts clock tower would chime the bells just like Big Ben in London. Queen Elizabeth Kindergarten opened on 19 May 1938, then there was the Crosier Club with its tennis courts (for staff members), Scout Hall and a gymnasium.

Katherine Graham was buried in the graveyard that was built to serve the school, and it was on 15 May 1942 that Dr Graham died, the same day, and yet so many years apart. We would always visit the graves of Dr and Mrs Graham during the school's birthday celebrations.

To help with finances Dr Graham set up committees of interested people in Cawnpore, Allahabad, Asansol, Bombay, Delhi and of course Calcutta. Other constructions were the Steele Memorial Hospital, The Watson Infectious Ward, and a store and bakery where fresh bread was baked and delivered to the cottages. Then there was Yule House (1913), the store manager's residence, Jubail House, the principal's residence near the chapel, and there were other practical buildings and constructions to make our lives happy and comfortable like the C.C. McLeod Swimming Baths where we had our annual swimming championships, one great reason we were all able to swim from an early age. I remember receiving a fried egg for breakfast after I managed to complete one length of the pool without any assistance. There was a big park called the Ronald Shay Park, which was quite large and flat as we would have our annual Sports Carnival with racetracks, hurdles, swings and other sports activities such as footy (soccer) and hockey, though I do not remember ever playing cricket. The whole compound was about 500-600 acres which enabled us the freedom to play hide and seek games, and of course cross country running (called harriers).

This was part of the final program of the school's annual Sports Carnival, held in October or November. Unfortunately, some of us who stayed on the school compound or camped by the Riley River 5 miles south of the school, which was a great spot to practice fishing and running around in the freezing crystal-clear water, knew it was getting close to Going Home Day. That was when all the busses and jeeps would line up along the main office, and we would wave goodbye to our friends who were going home to their families for the winter school holidays. It would be almost three months before they returned in February for the start of the new year.

We were indeed fortunate each of these cottages housed up to 30 children, divided into two dormitories. Fifteen older boys or girls looked after and had charge of 15 younger children. There was a total of just over 500 boarders and maybe 100–150-day scholars from all over the district. On the compounds were teachers, house uncles and aunties and many other members of staff. At the time I was there in my later years was Mr Purdy, Mr Donald Ross was the headmaster, Rev Ewin G.S. Trail was the principal and after Mr Donald Ross left for a position in the USA, Dr James Minto was the new headmaster. One of my favourite teachers was Miss Hastings. She taught history and geography, my two favourite subjects. She married Mr Hill in The Kathrine Memorial Chapel, and we all had a big celebration as we would for the school birthday.

There were many domestic staff. Each cottage had a cook, and each cottage would have a teacher who would stay in the teacher's room. I remembered in my time, was Miss Jean Gillespie. We would have a barber come around once a month to give us the standard short back and sides, there were gardeners (malies) who worked alongside their wives (Kanchi or Ayah was their Nepalese or Hindi name for female workers who maintained the grounds and gardens), there was a general washroom for the whole school, and dhobis (laundrymen) who would collect the sheets and pillowcases from the cottages. There were many people working on the farm. Most of the labourers were Lepchas or Nepalese, and the main language spoken by them was Nepalese and Hindi and a sprinkling of Bengali as we were in the state of West Bengal.

At the time I was in the Homes, I was made to understand that I was an orphan and had no known other family than my two elder brothers Winston and Errol. Later, I was to meet another brother Donovan Oakley, he was my brother from a different father, who in my later years was protective of me, when I first left school and lived in the Birkmyre Hostel in Calcutta as a young lad. More of that part of my life in a later chapter.

One thing that stood out was the fact that none of us ever wore shoes, and we thought nothing of that as we all felt equal and free as a bird, until about 1962 when shoes became a part of the school uniform. There was a clothing store where all uniforms and repairs were conducted. We had a winter uniform, a summer uniform and a dress uniform that we would wear on very special occasions like visits from VIPs, such as then Prime Minister of India Jawaharlal Nehru and his daughter Indira Gandhi, who was to eventually become prime minister in the 1970s. We also had a visit from the Dalai Lama when he fled Tibet after the country was taken over by China, and for the homes' birthday celebration on 24 September of each year. We would all get buns and jellabies with smoked sweet tea, what a treat that was on 24 September each year. The whole school was encouraged to be there at the Crosier Club, including many members of staff and VIPs, and each cottage would form a circle, with the boys' cottages on one side and the girls' cottages on the other.

The homes were located above the town of Kalimpong. Nestled in the foothills at an altitude of some 1,200 meters or 4,100 feet was the town of Kalimpong at the foothills of the Himalayan Mountain range, stretching for some 2,000 miles to the north. The only way for the traders to travel was through two mountain passes called Nathu La and Jelep La. Kalimpong was once a staging post for trade and commerce between India, Sikkim, Bhutan and Tibet. The main means of travel for these merchants was by walking or using yaks and surefooted mules. They would have a bell around their necks and as a young child I would love to hear the echo of the bells through the mountains, hills and valleys, many days in advance of them getting into view, we would see them as tiny specks against the mountain sides.

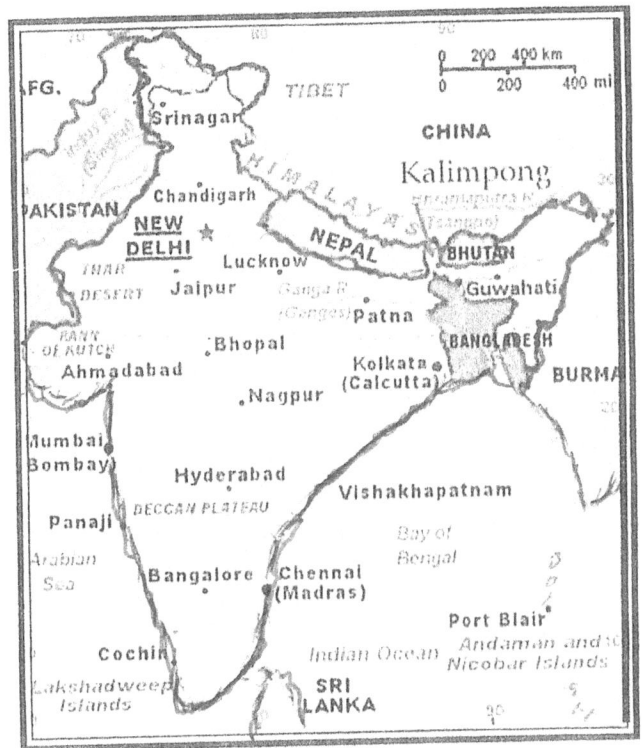

Map of India with location of Kalimpong.

Ray of Sunshine 10-year-old.

And the winner is Calcutta Cottage Front Row L-R Raymond, John Dempster, Back Errol Cooke, not sure? Robert Coutts.

Mt. Kanchenjunga.

John Sharman, Raymond Cooke & Denis Vellums, all in our Sunday best.

School Block, DGH Independence Day Parade on 15th August each year.

CHAPTER 3

Life in Dr Graham's Homes

I was admitted to The Homes on 14 August 1947, that made me 20 months old, along with my 2 brothers Winston George Cooke (dob 27 March1942) (Winston passed away in December 2005) and Errol Anthony Cooke (dob 11 October 1944).

On this day, the new country of Pakistan was created and chose to break away from India, who on the stroke of the midnight hour on 15 August 1947 became an independent country with close to 400 million people, with many languages, castes, creeds and religions joined to form one vast country. It was divided in two by the British to form a predominantly Hindu India and a predominantly Muslim Pakistan. As you can imagine there was a lot of bloodshed and murder on both sides of each border. It is estimated that close to a million people died and anything up to 10 million refugees on both sides with terrible suffering. Many lost their homes, and many families were separated from each other at the stroke of a pen. There was the absurd creation of Pakistan divided into two, West Pakistan was mainly formed by dividing Punjab, separated by more than a thousand miles, and East Pakistan was formed by dividing the state of Bengal into east and west. The east was Muslim, and the west was Hindu. This again was devastating as families were separated and driven from their homes. Again, there was a killing spree. I cannot imagine what it must have been like with three little boys travelling from Calcutta, now called Kolkata, all the way from Sealdah Station by train then crossing the Ganges River, which sometimes looked like a massive brown sea. The river is very sacred and held in reverence by the Hindu population. We would have scrambled across the ferry from one ghat (the pathway from the railway station to the steps, leading to the water's edge where the ferry was positioned) to the other ghat to catch another train to Siliguri. Then on a bus or a jeep for a distance of 80 km on a winding road for four-and-a-half hours. We would have passed two famous bridges, one being the Coronation Bridge that would take you to the other part of India, above East Pakistan into the fertile Brahmaputra River and its basin where many pulses, barley and rice grew and, of course, in the hills of Assam, tea was grown and exported all over the world. As June to September is the monsoon season, there was always the fear of landslides and the loss of the road, sometimes for weeks at a time, as makeshift emergency repairs were done to the roads. After the monsoon season the roads would then be shored up and repaired, ready for the next monsoon season the following year.

Personally, as a 20-month-old baby, all I do know from anecdotal and medical records is that I was in poor medical shape and suffering from malnutrition, with a bloated tummy and rickets. With skinny legs, I was unable to walk till I was about 4 or 5 years old. I was put, with my brother Errol, in Lucia King, which was a home for babies and toddlers, under the watchful eye of the Aunty Dulcey Penny. There were other schoolgirls who were being trained to be child nurses (this was the option for girls that were not academically qualified to progress on to the Senior Cambridge year 12 examination). I do remember being very happy and loved and cared for.

At the age of about 4 my brother Errol and I were transferred to Mansfield Cottage, which was a girl's cottage, as an experiment for mixed-gender schooling, under Aunty Eames and Aunty Hitchner. From there we were later transferred to Calcutta Cottage, which was the closest to the school on the boys' side and just below the Katherine Memorial Chapel. I do remember our house Aunty was Aunty Cussini. In the early part of the 1950s we had Mr Len and Mrs Kris Clemence as uncle and aunty, who had a daughter Christine, a son Alan and later another baby son Graham.

I do remember those days with affection and love from Uncle and Aunty Clements. My brother Errol and I were fortunate enough one year to go away for our school holidays with Uncle and Aunty Clemence and their family to Sahibgunge. Uncle Len Clemence was a military man and served in the RAF and was the father image we needed with discipline, and love we got from Aunty Clemence. They left the Homes after about 3 years. I was still a small chap when they left but I never forgot the love and kindness that they gave to us growing up without any parents of our own. I did keep in touch with him well into his 90s and he had a remarkable memory. I spoke to him on the telephone, and he remembered I was one of the three Cooke brothers. I was able to catch up with Aunty Clemence, in her late 80s, when she came for a holiday to Australia, with her travel companion and her daughter Christine and her husband Keith Lock. It was a wonderful reunion, and I will always treasure those memories.

A few of us children did not go home for school holidays. The school would close from mid-December through to late February the following year. Aside from the trip with Uncle and Aunty Clements to Sahibgunge, we were also fortunate that Uncle and Aunty Hopman took us to Chennai (Madras) during another one of these school holidays.

Our daily routine in the cottage began by being woken up by 6 am, usually with a bell or some loud shouting by Uncle and Aunty, then made our bed and had a wash before going to breakfast. There was always a quick round of chores before dressing into our school uniform. After a quick inspection of our fingernails and our hands and sometimes a quick check behind the ear, we then headed off to the chapel for a 15-minute devotion. This was on Tuesdays through to Fridays. Mondays were usually reserved for school assembly, and classes would resume at 8:30 am. The sound of the school gong would see us charging from one class or subject to another in an orderly fashion. Lunch was from noon to 1 pm and was always a dash to our respective cottages. I was lucky as Calcutta Cottage was the closest to the school. We were always hungry or as we in school would say "abs grubby". After lunch we would head back to school for the afternoon session until about 3:30 pm. After school there was usually an assortment of sports depending on the time of year like footy (soccer), hockey and running cross country, and of course we had to be back at the cottage for our evening meal. After washing up and tidying the dining rooms we would then do our homework for 1 to 2 hours depending on your grade. Sometimes we would break into songs like choruses, that was something we always enjoyed, as once a year there would be an inter-cottage singing competition. Other times, we would practice poetry, elocution and other training for the Duke of Edinburgh Competition held at the end of the year. The senior boys and girls plus the ones in the hostels would meet at the Science Block for their homework or night classes, supervised by some teachers. Lights out was usually about 9 pm.

I loved doing kitchen duties, that usually entailed waking up nice and early about 4:30 am. We had to light the chulia, which was a bucket with a grate and mud interior, usually gathered twigs or wood shavings from the workshop, below the art class at the end of the school playing fields. We had a box of matches, some newspaper and of course charcoal which was lighter than the steam coal. We would light the fire in preparation for Kupla, who was the Calcutta Cottage cook for at least 10 years that I was in Calcutta Cottage. After lighting the fire, we would make a cup of "cha" or tea for Uncle and Aunty, this was before 6 am and the cook would arrive and collect the beads of red-hot charcoal to start the main coal stove, that also served to provide hot water for use in the cottage for washing and our showers. The cottage cook would prepare breakfast, usually consisting of a plate of oatmeal porridge, or dhal or lentils as a soup with two slices of bread, and a cup of tea without sugar. Lunch consisted of rice and curry and dinner was usually a stew with assorted vegetables (pumpkin, squash, beans, chana dhal, potatoes, peas, brinjals, huge cucumbers, turnips) and of course meat, beef, pork or chicken depending on the supply from the farm. A vulnerable time was during the grace. This was when we had our eyes closed as we prayed, and it was an opportune time for those on either side to steal food from our plates. This was called survival skills, as in the movie *Oliver*. As a kitchen hand we were excused from other chores, so we usually peeled and washed the veggies for lunch and dinner. One benefit of working in the kitchen was we always had food, as we would also have to butter the bread with lard, one scrape on and two scrapes off as there was a limited supply of lard and margarine. Butter was reserved for our special treat, a slice of cake or fudge made from powdered milk or peanut brittle with peanuts and gur (molasses). These were specials and I remember trading my cake or sweets with boys who disliked veggies, for a week's supply of one portion of their pumpkin, squash, turnips or beans, so I had a roaring trade with my cake or sweets and always had a good supply. I learned these entrepreneur skills or qualities early in life.

I also enjoyed sewing and had a side trade sewing buttons on school and sports uniforms for a couple of annas to supplement my pocket money of Rs2 a month. This enabled me to buy all sorts of snacks from either the tuckshop run by Mr Kelly, or the boxwallah with his cream puffs. He was always good for tick (credit). He had a great memory of anyone that owed him money at the end of the month, when we would line up for our pocket money. Surprisingly Rs2 went a very long way just like an elastic!

I do remember that when I was about 7 or 8 years old, I developed bronchial asthma, and suffered seasonally, depending on wind conditions and pollen from all the flowers and plants with flowers. With this condition I had many stints in the Steele Memorial Hospital. I was always looked after well by Sister Cassidy and the trainee nurses. I would always volunteer to help in the kitchen or pantry with washing up after meals and other odd jobs. I was a regular patient over the years and my treatment included Benadryl, a beautiful, sweet syrup. That and a small ephedrine tablet seemed to work miracles.

I thoroughly enjoyed my life in the Homes and made many friends who became lifelong friends. We all had something in common, and each one of us has a unique story to share. I felt that my early childhood experience and a good Christian upbringing stood me in good stead for my life in the future.

My asthma progressively got worse, and the attacks were getting more regular. This all came to a climax on 14 August 1960. We all went down to the town of Kalimpong, about 5 miles down the hillside from Dr Graham's Homes, for the inter school footy (soccer) competition between other schools in the district. This was part of the celebrations for India Independence Day and was a highlight of the year for us.

Halfway through the game, amid all the screams of encouragement for the home's team, I began to feel an asthma attack coming on. I decided to head the 5 miles back up the hill, to the safety of hospital in the Homes.

I did not know how I eventually arrived at the hospital and to my delight, I just recently came to know, it was George Borthwick who carried me up the stone steps behind the Katherine Memorial Chapel. He recollected that he was already so exhausted once he got to the top of the steps, and then ran with me on his back all the way to the Hospital. I never got the opportunity to thank him then, but I do believe that I am writing this book because of his kindness and dedication in saving my life. I always remember George as a gentle giant, who came to my aid in school when confronted by a bully. My old school friend George is the author of the book, *My Name is*

George – This is my Story - A Story of Challenge and Life by George Anthony Borthwick QSM.

My friend George Borthwick.

He was one of my inspirations and he had faith in my ability to put my thoughts into words. George was with me in Dr Graham's Homes from the time I arrived till the time I left in 1960. We were also in the Birkmyre Hostel together during my years in Calcutta (Kolkata) before we left for our respective destinations in Australia and New Zealand. I did meet George again in 1974, and again when he visited us OGBs in Sydney, and have kept in touch with him ever since. That is the beauty of being from the DGH family. We can pick up where we left off even after 30, 40 or 50 years. Each of us have our own experience and unique ability to communicate with each other as no other alumni that I have been associated with.

When we reached the hospital, Sister Ruth Cummings, a missionary from Australia, was on duty and examined me. I was admitted, as my condition was not helped by the trip from the township, and I was in poor shape. I remember being placed in one of the dormitories with a curtain around me. I was finding it extremely hard to breathe and Sister Cummings assured me that I would be fine. She had rung the home's resident, Dr Rao from town, to come and attend to me. As he was examining me, my breathing was getting worse. To my recollection, I remember him telling Sister Cummings that my respiration was getting worse at 160 a minute, he then told sister Ruth Cummings (Smith), "We are losing him", and again, "We are losing him".

I then had the strangest experience, as I felt myself floating up to the corner of the room and looking down at Dr Rao and Sister Cummings, looking at me in the bed. It was 14 August 1960 when I was admitted in the hospital. I must have been in a bad way for I do not remember much of what happened after that. When I opened my eyes, I noticed it was a beautiful sunny day and I had been moved to a small room on the verandas looking towards the plains. Sister Ruth Cummings was there beside me holding my hand. My first words were, "Oh, today is a holiday. It is Indian Independence Day, the 15th of August". To my surprise she said in a calm voice, "No, today is the 20th of August and I have been by your side all this time". It took me a while to comprehend this. I had been in a coma for the last 5 days and I heard that the whole school was praying for me. She asked me if I was hungry, and I said I am starving. She disappeared to leave me to my own thoughts. When she returned, she came back with 2 fried eggs on toast. I remembered the last time I had a fried egg was when I swam the length of the swimming pool, that was my prize; it felt like a lifetime ago. I do remember that she continued to look after me, as arrangements were made for me to be transferred to continue my schooling in Kolkata (Calcutta).

On 4 October 1960 I was invited to the principal's home near the church, and he told me that because of my health, it was decided to send me to St Thomas Boys' School (established in the 1700s) in Kidderpore, Calcutta. It was then that I was advised that during my convalescence after my near-death experience, they had been trying to find suitable sponsors for my further education and boarding in the new school. He prayed with me and presented me with a bible as was the custom when pupils left the school. On the inside cover were the inscribed words:

"RAYMOND COOKE WITH EVERY
GOOD WISH FOR THE FUTURE"
signed Ewin G.S. Trail, Principal Dr Graham's
Homes, Kalimpong, dated 4 Oct1960.

The bible verses: Numbers Ch 6: vs 24-26:)

24: The Lord bless thee and keep thee; 25: The Lord make his face to shine upon thee and be gracious unto thee; 26: The Lord lift up his countenance upon thee and give thee peace".

Sister Ruth Cummings had knitted a red pullover for me as a gift and a coloured photograph was taken of me wearing this pullover, on my last day in Dr. Grahams Homes, Kalimpong. I still have that photograph framed on my desk till this day, as well as stored on my computer, as with many other school photographs in my OGB file.

Sister Cummings organised for me to come and spend my first Christmas from Kolkata (Calcutta) with her in Kalimpong. I had my first flight in an aircraft, a Dakota DC-3, and was sitting in a window seat overlooking the wing of the aircraft all the way to Bagdogra airport. When I did contact her after 30-40 years, she remembered me and said she had the picture of me in a red jumper she had knitted for me on her fridge. Since then, I have always rung her on her birthday on 29 June each year, knowing full well her birthday is 29 July, and we always have a good laugh about that. She is an inspiration and a God-fearing lady and has been blessed richly, with a wonderful family and a well-deserved retirement from the hard work on the farm with her late husband Arthur. We all miss him, and thank God for bringing him into our lives.

Calcutta Cottage with Uncle & Aunty Clemence – 1954.

School Concert 1955.

Calcutta Cottage with Aunty Georgina Sampson -1960.

DGH Birthday celebrations – buns, smoked tea and jellabies, in cottage groups, 24 September each year.

Uncle and Aunty Clemence and family in Sahibgunge India late 1950s.

Matron Cassidy & Sister Ruth Cummings (Smith)-1960.

Matron Cassidy, Sister Ruth Cummings (Smith),
Mr & Mrs Ipe and nursing staff-1960.

Raymond A Cooke 04.10.1960 – Farewell DGH, with my red jumper
knitted for me with TLC by Sister Ruth Cummings (Smith)

CHAPTER 4

St Thomas Boys' School days - Kolkata 1960-1963

I left the only Homes I had known, with all the love and care for the last 13 years on 04 October 1960. I was going to be 15 years old in a few months. I was anxious and apprehensive with this big move from my home to a big boarding school in a bustling city, the capital city of West Bengal.

I settled into my new life in St Thomas Boys' School in Kidderpore, Calcutta, located right next to the Calcutta Zoo. Built in the 1700s, it was a huge boys' school. The principal was Mr Theo Vise and the headmaster was Mr Pratt. Adjacent was the girls' school, where the principal was Miss De Abro. I settled in well and being a friendly kind of chap, made friends easily.

As a student in St Thomas Boy's School, I was quite taken aback when at assembly on Monday morning, it was announced. "Would all free boarders, come to the front to collect your toiletries". I had never heard the term of free boarder in my life and felt degraded as I approached the front of all the assembled students to collect our toiletries, like soap, toothbrush, toothpaste and shoe polish.

When I was in Dr Graham's Homes, neither I nor any other student wore shoes. One of the reasons, I was given to understand much later in life, was that Dr Graham wanted all the children of the Homes to be treated as equals no matter what their standing in life. I believe to this day that it was indeed one of the most humane ways in which to treat all people with mutual respect and understanding, no matter their religion, caste, language, colour of their skin or creed. Many of us children who were sponsored by the Christian Children's Fund (CCF) would write letters to our sponsors advising them or our academic achievements, sports, likes and activities we were involved in. We would also thank them for sponsoring us and giving us the opportunity to study and live life to the fullest, with a good Christian upbringing and principles.

I was selected to work in the Anglican Church as a server, which meant an early rise to prepare the church for the local faithful from the retirement home who attended the morning service conducted by Canon Robinson. I was eventually confirmed in the Anglican church. One of my duties in the church was for Sunday services procession, to carry the cross, followed by Canon Robinson, the principal Mr Vise and members of the choir. I also had to get the wafers and wine ready for the communion.

Over the one or two years that I diligently did my duty as a server, I hardly, if ever, tasted the wine during communion, as the chalice would be put to your lips, but slipped away before one even got a chance to taste the wine. Being a teenager and probably inquisitive to taste the wine, one Sunday I came nice and early to organise for the communion service. I got the wafers and took out the wine that was put into the chalice. I looked around and no one was there. I had decided to try and taste the wine. As I put the decanter to my mouth and tasted the beautiful pure port wine, I heard a cough behind me and nearly dropped the decanter. There was Canon Robinson. I had been sprung and I apologised to him, but he rebuked me severely and warned me that this was very serious, that I could be excommunicated from the church. I did not realise the significance of my crime, but one consolation was that I was taken off the roster. I was able to sleep in again, no more early morning calls to worship.

One thing I do remember is that while I was in St Thomas School, I was eager to make a way for myself, and realised that I had some talents that I could use to my advantage. As you can imagine in a 3-storey block dormitory filled with nearly 500 borders, there were boys of all ages. Each Saturday and Sunday the sport of cricket was a part of the sports curriculum of the school. In those days there were no zipper in trousers, but a series of buttons. I learned to sew buttons when I was in Dr Graham's Homes, so I took the opportunity to make my own pocket money. I would sew buttons at 4 annas a piece. (16 annas made one rupee.) In the hopes that my job and cash flow would continue, I would sew the buttons with only one or two loops so that the buttons would not stay attached long. My unsuspecting "customers" kept coming back.

I had made a steel box in the welding shop and each time I either sewed a button or did some ironing, I would place these coins into that box.

I was an average student and after completing year 10, was placed in the technical department where I learned to become a welder. Coincidentally it was exactly 3 years to the day on 4 October 1960 under very sad circumstances, and with my deepest gratitude, that my sponsors in the USA were killed in a car accident, so not having a sponsor meant I had to leave.

When I left the school, I took this box with me and to my delight I saw that over the last three years I had managed to save Rs265, enough for me to purchase my own brand-new Raleigh bicycle, so that I could go to work and for sightseeing in Calcutta. I was given a job in the Kalimpong Home Products bakery with a salary of Rs40 each month. Out of that I paid my subsidised dues in the Birkmyre Hostel in Middleton Row in the heart of the city of Calcutta, which was Rs10 a month for a bed in a dormitory and 3 meals. What a deal, even in those days! The Birkmyre Hostel was a gift from Sir Archibald Birkmyre to the boys of Dr. Graham's Homes. This place gave one a sense of security and comfort, and a chance to settle into the working environment, and was quite central in the heart of the huge city. This gave one an opportunity to share our early working lives, and many friendships were cultivated there. This was a wonderful experience, as I had been to school with many of the boys who were staying there. We all worked in different areas of the bustling city of Kolkata (Calcutta), the capital in the State of West Bengal. This used to be the capital of India during the early stages of the British Raj.

CHAPTER 5

Meeting my parents for the first time

Before I left St Thomas Boy's School, I was approached by my geography teacher, who asked me if I knew anything about my parents, to which I replied "no", that I went to Dr Graham's Homes in Kalimpong when I was a baby and was told that I was an orphan. There was no history of my parents. He asked my full name and date of birth and where I was baptised. I told him I was born at Wellesley Street in Calcutta, West Bengal as it was known after independence. He said he may know who my parents were, which made me very inquisitive and happy at the same time, though a bit apprehensive. He told me that he had some connections in St Thomas Church in Middleton Row, Calcutta 16, and would try and check it out for me.

The year 1962 was a traumatic time in India and China's relations and there were incursions and a lot of military activity in Ladakh and the Kashmir Valley, at the north-western border with the armed forces of India and China. India at this time still had a dispute in Kashmir when the ruler of Kashmir, a Hindu, decided to join the new majority Hindu Country of India in 1947, after which there were constant border skirmishes between the two countries. The United Nations formed an LOC (Line of Control), monitored by military observers of the United Nations, that is still one of the longest military deployments of the UN. In the meantime, there was a full-scale war raging in the NEFA (Northeast Frontier Agency) now known as Arunachala Pradesh, on 20 October 1962. According to reports,

China had invaded India through NEFA and Kalimpong came in close proximity to the Chinese military forces (PLA) in the Tibetan Plateau, within easy striking distance of a very strategic region of India and cutting off the Indian Army from responding militarily through West Bengal and the rest of Assam in the East, known as a corridor, called the Chicken's Neck between Nepal, the new Indian state of Sikkim, Bhutan and the newly formed East Pakistan in 1947. This corridor was just 5 miles wide and needed to be defended at all costs by the Indian Army. It was feared that should fighting proceed through Nathu La and Jepa La Passes, then Kalimpong would be in grave danger, and it would be a major problem and tragic if the children of Kalimpong and other schools in the Darjeeling District became victims of the war.

It was during this time that all the children and schools in the District of Darjeeling were evacuated to the protection of their parents. Other children in Dr Graham's Homes that did not have a home to go to were evacuated to Gopalpur in Orrisa State south of West Bengal and the Bay of Bengal. Many children of Kalimpong had never been to a beach and this meant an ideal opportunity in them to swim and enjoy the beach. They were there for a full 6 months till the situation on the border had stabilized.

During this time my teacher had checked it out and was able to give me the information about my parents, who were George Cooke and his wife Lillian Cooke. They were living in Royd Street. I looked up the map and discovered this was close to Park Street and Middleton Row, where the Birkmyre Hostel was. I would catch a tram No 31 that would run along the huge maidan (park) where the Victoria Memorial was. I decided to visit my brother Donovan, in the hope of getting some pocket money. He would always give me Rs5 each month, or whenever I could get to make the trip. I would always remember his generosity and kindness toward me. Don lived in the Birkmyre Hostel, where I would later live as well, and he worked for the licence measure's which was a branch of the government in the port of Calcutta, in close cooperation with customs on the Hooghly River and Port of Calcutta. There was Freeschool St, Rippon St, Wellesley Street and Elliot Road, and this area of Calcutta was inhabited by the Anglo-Indian community.

I did not tell my brother Don about my parents but made my way to Royd Street and after walking for what seemed like hours, I plucked up enough courage to walk into a big chemist shop on the corner of Wellesley St and Royd St and ask if anyone knew of a George Cooke. To my surprise one of the ladies working there said she did know of someone by that name who lived in No 16. I was getting more and more excited and as I headed toward Elliot Rd and the tram line, I came across a second-hand book shop close to No.16. I went in and asked the owner if he knew a George Cooke. He told me he was just around the corner and pointed me to head through a narrow passage. I missed the entrance and there was a bigger gate close to the Assembly of God Church, which was No 18. My heart was pounding as I approached and knew I was in the compound of 16 Royd Street. I saw near the entrance to their door was a katia (timber and jute matting bed). I knocked on the tin shed door and a lady came out and asked me what I wanted. She would have been in her late 30s or early 40s. I told her my name was Raymond Cooke and I was looking for a gentleman named George Albert Cooke who could be my father. This lady, as I remember, appeared to have had a hard life. She had a fair complexion and was Anglo-Indian in appearance. She asked my name, and I told her I was Raymond Anthony Cooke, and was in Dr Graham's Homes in Kalimpong. She looked at me without any emotion and said, "I know who you are". I was shocked and surprised as she said, "I am your mother and George Cooke is your father". I noticed there was a young shy girl probably just 13 or 14 years old. I later found out she was my sister Judy Susan Cooke. I was stunned and did not know what to do or say, maybe emotionally I was not prepared. I did not feel any connection or affection. I did not know if I should kiss or hug her or maybe not. I did not know this person at all. Sadly, I felt no emotion, no connection or empathy, whatsoever, for this lady standing in front of me. I did notice the room was tiny, 6 feet by 6 feet, with a double bed, small cupboard with a wash basin on top, a little stove and a single light bulb hanging from the roof. I must say that it was spotless even though there was no toilet or washroom. There was a public toilet around the back, one can only imagine the smell and the unsafe hygiene condition.

There was not much I could say as I was still in shock. I asked her where George Cooke was, and she said he was probably in the government grog shop. I then asked her, "Is it okay if I wait?" She then asked me, "Would you like a cup of tea?" and I replied, "Yes".

My mother then mentioned that her mother Gladys May Oakley (1889-1975), my grandmother, lived just around the corner in the same compound in a flat. While waiting for my father, I asked if I could meet her. Without a word she took me around to her flat. I remembered when my granny came to the door that she was a well-dressed lady, had deep blue eyes, and strikingly white hair cut short. She was short in stature, but a beautiful lady, full of love. I immediately took a liking to her. She was so kind and gentle and listened intently to me as I was excitingly talking to her.

She seemed very relaxed, but as soon as she heard my father call out to my mother, she hesitated and told my mother, "You had better go to him, as he is probably drunk." That was my first impression of my granny, and I just could not wait to meet up with her again, as I had so much to ask her. I made a pact with her, asking, "Can I come and visit you?" to which without any hesitation, she replied, "I would love that, I love you, my grandson." Again, I was more than surprised as no one in my entire life had ever told me that they loved me, and for once I now felt I had someone to love. I had so much to catch up with, over all these years. I gave her a kiss on her forehead, and she hugged me in return. She said, "I hope to see you soon". To which I replied, "I cannot wait to see you again", and she gave me a big smile. I knew I had a friend for life.

My mother pointed to a man staggering through the passageway from the street and said, "That is George Cooke, your father". I did notice that he was drunk and was darker in complexion than my mother, sister or myself.

When he approached, I asked him if he was my father. He abruptly replied, "yes" and said, "I sent you to Dr Graham's Homes in Kalimpong, along with your two older brothers, Winston and Errol." He said that my sister Judy was evacuated from the school because of the war raging between India and China.

I knew that I had found my father, mother and younger sister, who was extremely shy. She did not say a word in all the time I was there, though at times she would glance at me and quickly look down.

I continued looking at my mother, father and sister, and could see and hear by their speech and the way they looked, this could actually be my parents and my younger sister.

Sadly, and strangely, I did not feel any affection or any connection with them. I did not bear any malice or hurt, because deep down inside I was able to understand that my parents were very poor, and that was the reason they had sent me to the Homes as a baby. I had so many questions I wanted to ask, but as my father was drunk, a lot of what he was saying did not make any sense to me. I bade farewell with the promise that I would come and visit them when I could afford a tram ride from Kidderpore. I was almost 17 years of age now and had been in St Thomas Boy's School Kidderpore for the last three years.

After all the excitement for the day, on the way back to school as I walked down Royd St, turned left into Free School, and again right onto Park Street, I noticed there were night clubs and across the road at the big intersection of Free School, St Park St and Middleton Row, at the corner, there was the confectionary shop called Flurry's. I walked all the way to the tram stop and headed back to school in Kidderpore. This was truly an extraordinary day, filled with emotion for the last 17 years I had searched and hoped this day would come, and here I was a member of a family I was yet to get to know. When I got home that night, I was so excited I just could not sleep and kept hearing the tigers, elephants, and all sorts of animal sounds from the Calcutta Zoo, just over the stone fence. Eventually I fell into a deep sleep.

My Grandmother Gladice May Oakley (BURROWS) 1889-1970.

My Father George Albert Cooke 1918-1975.

My Mother Lilian Muriel Cooke (OAKLEY) 1919-2001

CHAPTER 6

My life and work in Calcutta

I left St Thomas Boy's School on Tuesday 4 October 1963 after exactly 3 years. As I am an old boy of Dr Grahams Homes, I was taken in by Kalimpong Home Products, a confectionary business that had an affiliation with Dr Graham's Homes. This place gave us an opportunity to get a job and work after leaving school and heading into the wide blue yonder. I checked in to the Birkmyre Hostel on Middleton Row. I knew this place quite well as when in St Thomas Boy's School, I would catch the number 31 tram from Esplanade to Ballygunge and back as it passed right out the front of the school. As I said in the past I would visit my brother Donovan Oakley, and he would give me Rs5 on a regular basis. The Birkmyre Hostel was a gift from Sir Archie Birkmyre and built in 1927 for the welfare of boys when they left the protection of Dr Graham's Homes and started life and work in the city of Calcutta, a bustling city of close to 10 million people. Later in my life I came across a good book called *City of Joy* written by Larry Collins and Dominique Lapierre. This is a great book to understand the true feeling to be a part of this city. It was made into a blockbuster movie. Another great book, if you can get your hands on it from the library, is called *Freedom at Midnight*, by the same authors, about how Britain gave away an empire. These two books give you a great understanding of the history of India, leading up to 15 August 1947 and beyond, describing the immense challenges faced by the new Government of India and the freedom fighters that helped this come to pass. The first prime minister was Jawaharlal Nehru and of course there was the father of the nation Mohandas K. Gandhi. A lot has been written by this great man, who was determined to get independence for India and hoped it would be one nation for all religions, with many languages, an assortment of races, cultures and ethnic backgrounds blending into one homogeneous country living in peace and tranquillity, but that was not to be.

I started work in Kalimpong Home Products in the bakery at No 2 Totties Lane in Calcutta near the famous New Market with the hope of training to be a baker or as a steppingstone to future employment opportunities. I got stuck into my new employment and environment with the determination to make a better life for myself. Though at the beginning it took some time for me to settle down, especially during the summer months where temperatures would reach 40-45 degrees. Can you imagine how hot it would be in the bakery with the hot gas oven? We were limited to a maximum of 30 minutes and then 10 minutes of reprieve from the intense heat. The smell of fresh bread would waft through the neighbourhood in the early hours of the morning. This was usually done about 4 am, and then would be delivered to the Shop situated at No.2 Middleton Row, a busy thoroughfare leading to The Loretto House and Convent and St Thom's Catholic Church at the end of the street near the Birkmyre Hostel. We were open 7 days a week, and one of the busiest days were on Sundays, as many worshippers would attend the Sunday services. It was busy for us in the shop as there were 3 services in the morning and one in the evening. There were many customers for our confectionaries, compared to the prices at Flurry's Swiss Confectionary shop. We supplied fresh bread all over Calcutta and it was always a busy time. I really enjoyed working in the bakery and learned a lot from the senior boys.

While at the Bakery I decided to improve on my schooling and qualifications by attending a school in the evening at the Patel Secretarial College, on the corner of Wellesley St and Park Street. The completion of the shorthand and typing course enabled me to gain further employment at The Little Shoppe on Park Street, opposite to St Xavier's College on Park Street and next door to the Park Street Police Station. My monthly salary increased from Rs40 to Rs260, and I was now able to pay a higher boarding fee than the original subsidised Rs10 a month when working at Kalimpong Home Products. The Little Shoppe was run by an Armenian family headed by Mr Malcom Soukous, and his brothers ran the workshop in Rippon Street that produced lamps and all kinds of modern furniture. Mr Soukous had many friends in the Armenian community, and many of them were businessmen and women. They were a very close-knit community and spoke the Armenian language. He was a good boss to work for and I learned many new skills, especially in sales, home decoration, and renovations. I worked long hours from 8 am to anytime between 6 pm and 10 pm. I left The Little Shoppe after a few years on my own free will, as I was offered another job at Kalimpong Home Products. One of the good things that came out of this experience was the improvement in my communication skills and especially my typing ability, as these stood me in good stead when I migrated to Australia.

CHAPTER 7

Meeting my first wife Theresa

In late 1968, I had gone to a dance being held at St Xavier's College, and out of the corner of my eye I saw this young girl, all on her own. I plucked up enough courage to ask her if she would dance with me. I was happy when she obliged, and we spoke for a while. I asked her name and she told me her name was Theresa Shrives. She told me that she worked as a primary school teacher, and her aunty had brought her to the dance, in the hope she would meet a family friend who was supposed to come there. He was late and by the time he had arrived, I knew that she was someone special and I was attracted to her, and I promised to keep in touch. Theresa told me she lived with her Aunty Coco in a flat in Chowringhee Lane. I knew where that was, as it was just around the corner from the Kalimpong Home Products bakery. I decided to check out the place where she lived and went on the pushbike, I had bought with money I saved up sewing buttons and ironing when I was in St Thomas Boy's school. I managed to find the block of flats where Theresa and her aunty lived. After a couple of weeks, I asked the guard at the gate where this lady with her niece lived, and he told me they were on the 5th floor. I got on the old-type lift where there were steel sliding doors. I got up there and waited near the balcony overlooking the street below. After waiting a short while I saw this lady and the girl coming toward the front. The guard told them that I was there and would be waiting for them when they came up the lift since I did not know exactly where they lived. As Aunty Coco was opening her door, I approached them and both recognised me, but were a bit apprehensive. I introduced myself and asked if it was okay for me to see Theresa. We had a good chat and after a short while promised to keep in touch if it was okay. I left after an hour and agreed to meet again. By this time, I was now working at the Kalimpong Home Products shop on Middleton Row. I did not hear or see Aunty Coco or Theresa for a while. One Sunday morning I did see them as they passed the shop on their way to mass. I ran out to catch up with them and asked if I could accompany them, to which I was invited. After church I was invited to meet Aunty Coco's sister who lived a few doors away from the church. I met Mr and Mrs Zcherpelle and their daughter Iona. Iona and her husband Charlie had 2 girls, and they had a lady named Mary Elliot who looked after the two girls. Much later, I learned that Mary Elliot was Theresa's mother. Theresa used to look after the two girls in her spare time or when required. Our friendship grew and I mentioned to Theresa that I was making enquiries in regard to migrating to Australia. I asked Aunty Coco Beeby if I could marry Theresa and said I would like to try and sponsor her after I arrived in Australia. Theresa agreed and I asked if we could get engaged before I left for Australia. I had taken Theresa to meet my granny and they got on well. As the time got closer to my time to leave, I organised for my grandmother to be a witness to my engagement to Theresa on 16 April 1969. I met Theresa and her aunty on my last day and we went out for a Chinese meal together as a farewell. It was sad to say goodbye to the woman I had come to trust with my life, and I sincerely wanted her to be a part of my life for as long as we both lived. My last day in India was 17 April 1969, and I had to make the rounds to say my goodbyes. I went and saw my mother and father as they knew of my decision to leave India for the betterment of my future. My granny had moved from her flat in 16 Royd Street to St Mary's Home for the Aged some years ago, and I had spent many hours with her over the years. Granny Oakley, as she became affectionately known by me, had collected many stamps for me especially from India, dating back to well before Independent India, as well as Australia and the UK as she had family members in those countries. She passed her collection on to me, as she knew I love history and geography, and she seemed to know that I would continue her stamp collecting. I do remember when I was in my last year of school and I met her for the first time, I would help her separate her stamps from the paper backing. She would watch me with interest as I would get very excited when I would see many old stamps. That is something I have to thank her for: teaching me to take care of stamps and learn a lot of history and geography from them. I loved listening to her stories and getting so much anecdotal information about her family history and my family tree, and where I stood. She was from a large family. Her husband William Henry Oakley had died in 1926, when my mother and her sister Alice were six and four years old respectively, and she had sent my mother and her sister to Dr Graham's Homes, Kalimpong. My mother was an average student and did a course in Lucia King as a child minder or nanny. My Aunty Alice McGowen (Oakley) had completed a nursing course at The Steele Memorial Hospital in DGH and had married Hector McGowen. They lived in company quarters of Dunlop's Rubber and Tyre Company Pty Ltd, where he had a good position after working his way up from an apprentice. After many years they had a son Keith McGowen who had attended La Martiniere school in Calcutta. I lost touch with him over the years and the last I heard he had married and settled in New Zealand. My granny was a nurse by profession, and after the early death of her husband she went back to nursing and would work her way to be a matron at the Ranchi Hospital, in the state of Bihar. After retirement she continued to use her skills as a nurse, and she was a member of The Salvation Army. She was a wonderful Christian lady and dedicated the later part of her life to visiting slums all over Calcutta. She would give injections and help the children of the slums daily, up to the last day of her life. She always did her usual rounds and returned home to have an afternoon nap before heading for dinner in the dining room. I was given to understand that she died peacefully in her sleep at the age of 81 years old.

Raymond 18 Years Old in Calcutta.

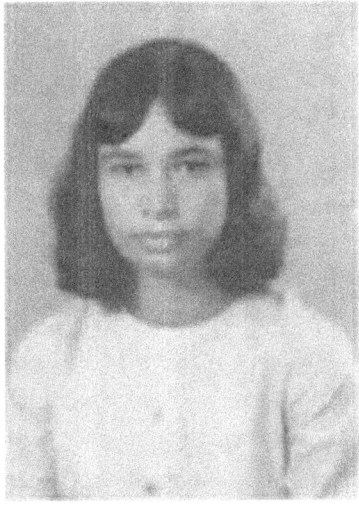

Theresa 18 years old in Calcutta.

CHAPTER 8

Leaving India for a new life in Australia

I left India for Australia on my Indian passport with US$8 in my pocket. We were not allowed to bring out any more money, as there was a restriction on currency by the Reserve Bank of India and you had to get a special permit stamped and authorised on the last page of your passport. I had a friend who worked in the Swiss Air office who wanted to give me a good experience on my flight to Sydney, Australia. I dutifully sent my brother a telegram to advise him of my ETA in Australia, scheduled to be 7 am on Saturday 19 April 1969. As the big Swiss Air aircraft started down the runway, I was a bit nervous and apprehensive. I was a young man of 23 leaving all that I knew and treasured behind me, as the aircraft gained altitude and my life of the past was speeding behind me. My first stop was Bangkok airport in Thailand. When I arrived, I noticed that there were many military personnel from the US Armed Forces stationed in Vietnam on R & R. After a few hours in the terminal building waiting for my connection flight on Cathay Pacific to Hong Kong, I learned that before our flight could leave, I had to pay a US$2 airport/departure tax. Our flight was called for Hong Kong. It was a hot and sweaty day, and we had to line up on the tarmac to enter the aircraft, a huge Boeing 707. I settled into my seat, and through sheer luck or planning by my friend in Calcutta, I managed to get a window seat. I was fascinated as I watched the aircraft speed down the runway, which seemed to take forever. Finally, the front of the aircraft began to rise and in a matter of minutes were heading further away from India. After a couple of hours, we arrived in Hong Kong, and I remember distinctly that as our aircraft was gradually coming in to land, there were apartment blocks on each side of the runway. On arrival in Hong Kong Airport, I noticed television screens beaming live pictures. I was totally engrossed, as I had never seen a TV in my life. Again, there was not much of a wait for my connecting flight on a Lufthansa aircraft to take me on my next flight to Singapore. Once more I had to pay another US$2 airport/departure tax. I had not been advised that I would have to pay these taxes and my funds were dwindling away. One thing I found great was the variety of food and snacks and, of course, Coca-Cola. Soon we arrived in Singapore, and it was still 18 April. I was given to understand that the flight to Sydney would be a long overnight flight. Though daunted by this news as most of the previous flights were a couple of hours each, this was one experience I was eagerly looking forward to. It was getting late and eventually at about 10 pm we began boarding our Singapore Airlines flight on my final leg. I checked to make sure I still had my passport and had paid the final airport/departure tax of US$2 leaving me with just the remaining US$2. I had a small brown cardboard suitcase with a very limited amount of clothes and all my life's valuables like photographs and my stamp collection. Our flight was called by the Singapore airline hostess, and we queued to board our flight. I put my suitcase above me in the locker but hung on to my passport and my remaining US$2. The flight took off on time and we had just taken off when the meals and beverages arrived. I was hungry as I had been travelling all day and was now on the last leg of my amazing journey and a change of life. Before we settled into the flight after our meal, we were given blankets, as it was getting quite cold as the air conditioning was turned on high. Early in the morning about 4:30 am we were woken up and given a hot towel, and breakfast arrived with a nice hot cup of tea. We landed at 7 am on 19 April 1969. I proceeded to Customs and Immigration and after getting my passport stamped with permission to settle in Australia, I was whisked through to the exit.

At last, I had arrived at my destination As I came out to the big hall, each and every one had someone to greet them. I waited with apprehension as there was no one there to greet me. I had US$2 in my pocket, and my small suitcase that I still have to this day. I asked a few people if they knew the best way to get to Summer Hill, where my brother Donavan lived.

He was supposed to collect me from the airport and take me to his home. Unfortunately, I found out later the telegram advising of my full itinerary and arrival was received a week after my arrival.

I was scared and was not sure what I was supposed to do, as I did not have a phone number to contact him. All I had was his address in Summer Hill. I came out of the Sydney Kingsford Smith Airport (today known as Sydney Domestic Airport) and proceeded to walk down O'Rierdon Street in Alexandria, towards the Redfern Railway Station. It was about 7:30 am on Saturday 19 April 1969. As I walked down this busy street, I noticed many factories and manufacturing businesses.

I noticed that there was a "vacancy" sign displayed at the main gate. I thought to myself this looks like an opportunity to see if I could try and secure employment. I stopped in front of a busy looking place called Austral Bronze Crane Copper Industries. I knocked on the glass of the security guard's office. He reluctantly approached, as he had to put his newspaper down, and in a stern voice he asked me, "What do you want?" I told him I saw a vacancy sign at the gate and would like to apply for a job. After a bit of persuasion, he said that even though it was a Saturday he would check if the personnel officer was in. To my delight, it turned out that Mr Smith, the personnel officer, was in his office. I felt that God was looking after me and had seen me through the ordeal of travelling halfway around the world in the last 24 hours without any hiccups. Finding the job opportunity, I was looking for was just "icing on the cake".

I was directed to go past No 1 and 2 Mills and to No 3 Mill where his office was. An elderly gentleman greeted me. He was cordial and kind enough to give me his time. He spoke with a friendly but distinctly Australian accent. I placed my little suitcase down and he pointed me to a seat opposite him. He then proceeded to ask me a series of questions, though I found it difficult to fully comprehend his accent. It took me back to the friends I had made when I worked in The Little Shoppe in Calcutta, when we renovated the Australian High Commissioner's Office. I had the privilege of meeting some nice friendly Australian staff working there, who had graciously assisted me in my decision to subsequently call Australia home. Mr Smith spoke of his WWII war experience in Calcutta, India as an Australian serviceman. He finally got down to the subject of why I was there. I told him I had just arrived this morning from India. He must have seen the determination in me as an asset to his company, and asked me what I wanted. I told him that I was prepared to do any honest job. I had experience working in an office and had attended night school to complete a Pitmans shorthand and typing course. He proceeded to open the blinds of his office that revealed the extent of a variety of huge machines and casually asked, "Would you be able to operate these machines?" I looked at them and replied, "I am willing to learn, and it probably would be a piece of cake". He chuckled, came back to his desk, and asked me, "When could you start?" to which I replied, "Now". He asked me to come back at 3 pm for the afternoon shift. He told me that the factory operated 24/7 on 3 shifts, the morning shift worked from 7 am to 3 pm, the afternoon shift began at 3 pm and went to 11 pm, and the night shift worked from 11 pm to 7 am. I had worked these hours when I worked in the bakery doing my apprenticeship as a baker. Then the strangest question of all was, "Do you speak English?" to which I replied, "I thought we have been speaking in English for the last 30-40 minutes". He had a good laugh and then explained to me that many of the workers were refugees from many countries in Europe, namely Hungary, Czech Republic, France, Portugal, Slovenia, Germany, Italy, Yugoslavia, Poland, Greece, Russia and of course people from Great Britain. They had left their homeland to find an opportunity to better their shattered lives after the conclusion of the Second World War. Many of them could not speak good English. He said it was "mullah" (money) that brought these people here, to which I had a blank expression on my face. He laughed and said in a very Australian accent, "pie die is on Thursdie" which really meant pay day is on Thursday!!! He told me the base rate of pay would be about $65 a week but with overtime I could expect to get between $75-$80 each week. I knew I had the job well and truly in my hand. I thanked him for his time, then he asked me if I would be prepared to work in the office as I had typing skills. The pay would be less, without overtime, but a 9 am-5 pm working day. I replied, "I would, but first I would like to get some experience in the factory before heading to the office", to which he agreed.

This company manufactured, among other things, strips of metal to produce radiator coils for the automobile industry in Melbourne. They also manufactured aluminium foil at .3mm thick by 1 meter wide by 1,000 meters long strips, all started from aluminium or copper ingots that were heated in furnaces and then processed through pressing machines and finally a cleaning process that bathed the metals in a water-diluted sulphuric acid bath and they eventually went to the strip mill that cut copper, brass and aluminium into strips. And they had another plant in Concord and Penrith which made plumbing supplies.

    I was delighted and after shaking his hand, left with a burden off my mind and went back to the front gate, where I thanked the guard at the gate and promised to see him for the afternoon shift.

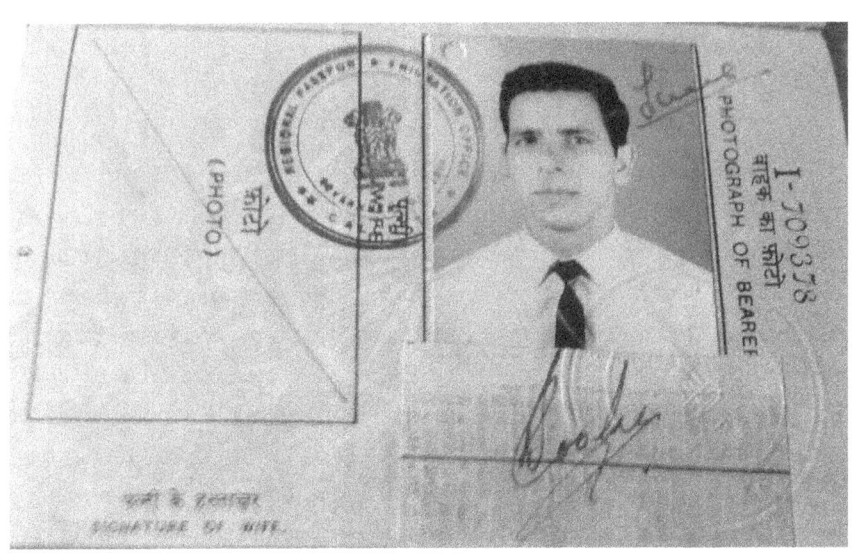
My Expired Indian Passport R. A. Cooke.

CHAPTER 9

Arrival and work experience in Australia

I caught a taxi to my brother Donavan (Don)'s home in Summer Hill, not knowing how I was going to pay for it, as I only had US$2 in my pocket. I was granted a temporary visa until I could apply for permanent residence, which in those days was not a big problem, if you had a job to support yourself and were not a burden on the taxpayers. I arrived at the address that had been communicated to me. The taxi fare came to $2.20. I paid the driver the US$2 that I had in my pocket. He asked me for the balance, and I told him, "I have just arrived as a new migrant, I do not have any more money". He was quite indignant and asked me to pay the full fare, to which I again explained that was all the money I had, but I would ask my brother if he would wait. He abused me by saying, "These wogs come to this country and don't even have money" and took off, leaving me at the footpath. I proceeded to my brother's house, which was a flat on the ground floor. I knocked at the door, and he opened it and was shocked to see me standing there. He asked me why I had not notified him of my intended arrival. I told him I had sent him a telegram to advise him of my itinerary, but obviously it had not arrived.

He advised me that he had organised for me to stay in a boarding house run by a lady. Don himself had stayed there before he got married on 29 December 1965. I got to meet his wife Charmaine and their 3-year daughter, Delphine.

Angelique's Boarding House was on Railway Street in Petersham, which was an area then settled by many Italian families. I found Mrs Angelique to be a very nice, warm and caring person. I was not alone as there were other OGBs there who had arrived before me. I would have a room with a single bed, dresser and cupboard, and would have to share the common bathroom, kitchen, dining room and laundry at the back. This all suited me fine, and reminded me of my good old days in Dr Graham's Homes and the Birkmyre Hostel in Calcutta (Kolkata). The rent was to be paid in advance at $10 per week. I borrowed $20 to pay my first week's rent as well as for transport by train and bus, as advised by some of the chaps at the boarding house. I would have to catch a train from Petersham, via Stanmore, Newtown, McDonald Town and get off at Redfern Station. Then climb up the stairs and turn right and walk 100 yards and again right, and walk a further 50-100 yards, before I came to the bus stop. Then I had to catch bus No 109 to Alexandria. On my first trip I had to check with the bus driver to tell me when to get off the bus. He was familiar with the factory as the bus stopped opposite the front gate of Austral Bronze Crane Copper Pty Ltd, a huge factory of more than 300-500 men on each shift.

I gradually got the hang of things and was quite happy working. It was a friendly environment and each of us workers were there to make a living and look after our families. I had decided to have my evening meal, at a nominal cost, at brother Don's home in Summer Hill, just a mile or two away. Being a young and energetic man, I loved the exercise, and looked forward to the company and conversation with his family, Charmaine and her mother, and getting to know my niece Delphine. Charmaine was a good cook, and I enjoyed the Indian cooking and meals graciously provided. I will forever be indebted to Don for sponsoring me to come to this country and give me the opportunity to fulfil my dreams and aspirations for my life.

Ray of Sunshine in Australia -1969.

CHAPTER 10

Arrival of Theresa from India and our marriage

I continued to work at Austral Bronze Crane Copper and submitted the paperwork to sponsor my fiancé Theresa on the grounds of spousal reunion. In the meantime, she applied for her Indian passport, and I would ring her from Mrs Angelique's phone in the boarding house. In those days, one had to book an overseas call through an operator, and calling India was quite a challenge. A 3-minute person to person call would cost about $10, and we would be interrupted by the operators many times. So, I learned to write all my points on a paper and try my best to stick to the list I had made, as we had so much to discuss.

As Theresa was a Catholic and I was confirmed Church of England, to marry her I had to attend catechism classes with Father Larkey of St Thomas Catholic Church, near Lewisham Hospital and Lewisham Railway Station. Each week I would attend these classes faithfully. As the time got closer for her arrival, I contacted my old boss at Kalimpong Home Products, whose name was Mr. Clarence Cooke. He had paid for my airfare of Rs5,000 when I left India. I opened a bank account where I would transfer funds on a regular basis, with all the overtime and 12-hour shifts, to repay him the loan. He was a very kind and generous man. I approached him again for Theresa's airfare. He knew I was good with money and honest to my "word". He agreed to pay her airfare which was another payment of Rs5,000. I continued to work hard and repay my debt to him. The paperwork was being processed and I was seeing the arrangements coming together. Once all the documentation and procedure came into fruition, my promise of 6 months to achieve this was becoming a reality.

It was time I started looking for a 1-bedroom flat and slowly began to furnish it with the basics required for us to make a home. I found a partly furnished flat at Palace Street in Lewisham, just a few streets away from the boarding house I was staying in. We organised the date for our marriage as 04 October 1969, a Saturday at 4 pm. I had invited my brother Don and his wife Charmaine and my niece to our wedding, but at the time she was pregnant, and her baby was due any day. We decided to go ahead with our original plans and Father Larkey said he would get a couple to witness our wedding as we did not have any family to be present. I had organised for Theresa to stay at the YWCA in the heart of Sydney before the wedding. She was arriving on 24 September 1969. I paid the deposit and waited for all God's plans to take place.

September 24th arrived, and I was at the airport nice and early in anticipation of her arrival. My heart skipped a beat as she appeared behind the glass exit and walked down the ramp to my waiting arms. I was overjoyed to see her and thanked God for delivering her to me. She also had a small suitcase with a few clothes and odds and ends. We caught a taxi and headed to the YMCA in the city in Liverpool Street, and checked her in. In those days, guests were not allowed to proceed past the foyer. After Theresa had found her room and settled in, we headed to Bathurst Street where there was a little sandwich shop run by a couple from Russia. Theresa was a very shy person by nature, and after ordering our breakfast, I began chatting with the owners who spoke in broken English. We got on well and I told him that we had just arrived from India and were hoping to get married soon, but my wife-to-be was staying at the YWCA, and I was staying in Lewisham. After listening to this they asked me, "Does Theresa have any experience working in a sandwich shop?" They said they were getting old and needed a reliable person to help in the shop, especially during breakfast and lunch time. The hours would be from 7 am to 3 pm each day. We were not too sure what the salary would be. After discussing our good fortune, between Theresa and I, we agreed that Theresa would start work the next morning nice and early. Again, that was God's hand working in our lives and placing such opportunities in our direction. Theresa started work the following day, and I would keep in touch via telephone each evening, depending on my shift. Theresa was alone and afraid of what lay ahead for us.

I went and saw Father Larkey at St Thomas Catholic Church and told him that Theresa had arrived. I handed over her passport, and when he saw the date of her birth advised me that we needed to get a parental permission, as the legal age for marriage was 21 years old. Theresa was just 20 and therefore would require a judge to give permission. I did not know of any lawyer or legal representative, and he advised us to go to the court in the City of Sydney and seek the advice of a magistrate or judge. The next day we walked into a courthouse in the city and asked the sheriff or security person, "Can we see a judge?" I explained our predicament. He was a kind elderly gentleman and after speaking to some lawyer, promised us that we could see a magistrate, as we did not require a judge. We were called in to the court and after swearing in, he asked Theresa, "Do you wish to get married?" and she replied, "Yes". He asked, "Do you have any parents?" She said to him, "I am an orphan. I have just arrived all the way from India to marry this man. This man was known to me in India, we had got engaged, and he had sponsored me on the grounds that we would get married". We told the magistrate that it was Father Larkey of the Catholic Church in Lewisham that had discovered the problem of age requirement. No one had told us this requirement. After he verified our stories, he gave us a signed and sealed letter, giving us permission to marry. The big day came on 04 October 1969 and our wedding was scheduled for 3:30 pm. We were asked to give a donation to the couple from the congregation who were witnesses to our marriage and a fee to Father. We had caught a taxi from our flat at Palace St, Lewisham to the church, and asked the cab driver if he would wait? "No worries, mate" was his reply, and it was all over in 10 minutes. We caught the same cab home. The taxi fare was $6. I was on the night shift, and after we had a Chinese dinner, I headed off to work by train and bus.

We lived in that flat till early 1971, when I sponsored my brother Errol to come to Australia. We had no option but to move to a bigger, two-bedroom flat, as we discovered to our delight that Theresa was pregnant, and we needed a bigger flat. We moved to a 2-bedroom partly furnished flat on Wardell Road in Lewisham. We were quite happy there. On the evening of 21 September 1971, Theresa went into labour, and we had to catch a bus to the King George V women's hospital in Camperdown. We were financially struggling and the only option we had was to catch a bus to the hospital. A little later my brother Errol came to keep me company. In those days one was not allowed to be with your wife when she goes into labour. The room we were waiting in had no heating and a couple of cheap armchairs. As the night came upon us, we kept asking the nurse how long it was going to be. She said, "should be 30 minutes to an hour". Finally, at about 5:30 am we were tired and hungry and dying for a cup of coffee. We asked the nurse, "Is it okay for us to walk to Newtown Station, to get a cup of coffee?" She said, "Yes". We headed off down the road to get our coffee and headed back to the hospital only to be told by the midwife, "Your wife Theresa has given birth to a beautiful, healthy baby girl, Ingrid Geraldine Cooke, 6 lb 12 oz at 6:20 am". She took us to where Theresa was and handed me this tiny baby in my arms. I was overjoyed as I held our baby in my arms. After a few minutes, she congratulated and ushered us out, advising us to go home and get some sleep. It was time to head off home for a good sleep, "Ha, a typical man!!!" I was now a father, and a happily married man, with the responsibility of looking after my wife and a baby girl. As new parents and without any family support, it was very difficult, and we had to learn about parenting the hard way.

Where Theresa worked, the Russian couple were willing to help to look after Ingrid for 18 months, while she continued to work there. In the meantime, I had been transferred to the Concord branch of Austral Bronze. It was easy to get there. I would hop on a train to Burwood then rush to catch a bus (as there was such short time to catch this connecting bus) to be at by work by 8 am and I finished work at 5:30 pm. This was a norm for all of us working in the office, to run to catch the bus that took us to Burwood railway station. As it was a short ride home, I would always walk in the front door by 6 pm.

I worked as a payroll clerk, with a staff of 4 and the personnel officer Ray Galbraith who was our boss. We handled all payroll enquiries and checked the list each month of those people that were to be retrenched in the following months.

By now we had moved to another comfortable 2-bedroom flat, close to Lewisham Station. I loved the job and had not taken any time off work. We still had our debts to pay and now the responsibility of bringing up a child. We were happy and settled in our new role as parents. We would happily go for walks usually on a Saturday or Sunday, from Lewisham all the way to the Sydney Opera House, that was then under construction near the Sydney Harbour Bridge.

It was on Friday 18 June 1972 that I saw my name on the list to be retrenched in September. I was flabbergasted and rang my boss Ray Galbraith, who was on leave. I told him the news and he told me, "Do not worry, you have a lot of leave up your sleeve" (meaning I had time to look for another job??). I had not taken any leave since 1969. Those were the days one could accumulate your annual and sick leave.

Dinner at Summer Hill -1969.

Raymond and Theresa – Christmas 1969.

Theresa and Raymond with our niece Delphine Oakley -1969.

Theresa's Mother Mary (Kani) With Carmalene & Lizzette in Perth 1970s.

CHAPTER 11

My RAAF Career Begins

I had become an Australian citizen on 31 July 1970. I got on the phone and rang the recruitment office on Friday at lunchtime and they told me to come to the recruitment office nice and early on Monday 20 June 1972.

I was one of the first ones there at 5:30 am, and at 6 am we were called in for medical examinations and a whole battery of tests, physical, psychological, aptitude, and English written tests. They looked at all our references, and at about 10:30 am we were all called into a big hall and then we were separated. Those who were rejected were asked to leave. At 11:00 am an officer and a warrant officer came into the hall, and we swore our allegiance to the Queen and country. Our first official order was to have a haircut, as soon as we left, after collecting our travel warrants for the train trip to Melbourne on the *Spirit of Progress* that night at 8 pm, along with meal vouchers for when we arrived in Melbourne. We would arrive in Melbourne the following morning and had a free day there, before we caught the *Overlander* to Adelaide that night.

When I was in India, I tried to join the Indian Air Force, but was rejected for some silly reason, that I had one leg a half-inch shorter than the other. I do not know to this day, which one is shorter. I was disappointed. I asked the wing commander, who was the medical officer, "Have you heard of Squadron Leader Douglas Bader?" His reply was, "Who was he?" I then advised him that he was a RAF pilot who had lost both his legs and had artificial metal legs after a flying accident. He had then learned to fly again, became a RAF ace fighter pilot, and was responsible for shooting down many enemy German aircraft, during the Battle of Britain. Later in the war he had been shot down, captured and escaped as a prisoner of war. A movie had been made about him called *Reach for the stars* to which he replied, "I have never heard of him". I gave up!!!

Theresa was quite shocked when I told her I was successful in joining the Royal Australian Air Force and was leaving that evening for my recruit training in Adelaide. I had signed for a 6-year contract with the RAAF starting immediately. I told her that I was not sure when I would be back. Our baby girl Ingrid was only 9 months old. There was a fear at the back of her mind that I could be posted to Vietnam, as the war was still ongoing, and Australia had a military contingent and commitment there. I felt I had a guaranteed job for the next 6 years. I knew this was my passion and I could make a career out of it.

While in Melbourne that free day, I made it a point to visit Mr Cooke who had migrated to Australia with his wife and 3 children. He was so delighted to see me and thanked me for being so prompt with the payments, as he had trusted me with $1,000 for both my wife's and my air passage to Australia. I am always indebted to him for his kindness and generosity. It was really a great experience to spend the whole day with him and the family before catching the *Overlander* train to Adelaide. We would be met and driven by bus to RAAF Base Edinburgh to do a 12-week recruit training. I became part of IRTU Recruit Course 1176. The base was east of the city heading toward Victoria and the NWS border.

After the train journey from Melbourne to Adelaide overnight we were met at the station by a severe looking warrant officer and a few senior NCOs, who yelled and barked at us to hurry up and collect our luggage and stand into line. There were about 50-60 new recruits. We were totally confused and did not understand the commands. Finally, we all settled down and we were herded onto buses for the trip to the RAAF Base Edinburgh, close to the new satellite city of Salisbury on the outskirts of Adelaide, the capitol of South Australia. On arrival at the base, we were advised that our first order was to proceed to the barber's shop to get a haircut. I thought I was okay as I had shaved my hair off in Sydney before I left, as we were instructed to do as our first order after signing on the dotted line for the next 6 years. That turned out to be a smart move as during the whole period I was at Number

One RAAF Recruiting Unit, not once was I ordered to have a haircut. I think the warrant officer must have had a share in the barber's shop, as he sent many recruits to have haircuts each week.

I discovered that I was one of the oldest guys on course. I was 23 going on 24, and the average recruit was 18 years old, and many had never left home in their lives without being chaperoned by one of their parents or older siblings.

The first day was spent going from one store to another collecting our kit: GP boots, joggers, socks, underpants, singlets, T-shirts, slouch hat, beret, webbing belt and two pairs of blue overalls and to hold all this gear we got a big blue duffel bag. We were sorted out into groups of 24-30 and taken to our huts called igloos. To my surprise they were quite large and there were beds lined up on each side. Each block had their own toilet and bathroom for washing and showering, and at the very end there was a small room for the corporal drill instructor (DI) assigned to each group of men. Our DI was CPL Don Smithers. He was loud and kept an eye on us. We were shown around the camp, all the many igloos that were around, and of course the parade grounds, the gymnasium, football fields and warned of out-of-bounds areas, i.e., the women's quarters. They were very similar to ours but were kept a good distance away.

It was time for lunch, and we were all lined up like cattle. The food was great, and the servings were more than adequate, after all there were almost 1,200 troops on the base and 1RTU was only one of the units. After lunch we were rounded up and taken to show the other facilities. There was a pub for the recruits, some big hangers that were used for church services, a movie hall, a swimming pool and other amenities. After all the running around, we finally had to go to the medical section for a medical assessment and an update of our medical records. After that we were escorted back to our billets as they were called. There were so many dotted around, it took a while to acclimatise and get our bearings. It had been a long first day and it was almost 17:00 hours and were told to go to our billet, change and get ready for dinner between 18:00 hours-19:00 hours. Breakfast was between 06:00 hours-07:00 hours, lunch was between 12:00 hours-13:00 hours and we had to be at the parade ground by 07:30 hours.

After dinner we went back to our billets and prepared for the next morning. As we were told, we had to make our beds, polish our boots, and dress in our overalls with the bottoms tucked with rubber bands and into our boots.

Bang! Bang! Bang! Then we heard the DI scream, "Wakey, wakey, rise and shine!!! Hands off c***s and put on socks". It was pitch dark, freezing and just 05:00 hours. Winter had settled nice and early that year in Adelaide. We were told to be ready for inspection in front of our beds at 05:30 hours. We all had to rush to have showers, brush our teeth and make our beds, and be all dressed and ready for our first inspection. Sharp at 05:30 hours we were ordered to stand to attention as our Sergeant Collins along with Corporal Smithers would conduct the inspection. He marched up and down, looked at each of us and got us to yell our names. He informed us he was our platoon commander, and we were to be on first name basis from today, we would call him Sergeant and he would refer to us as ACR (air craftsman recruit) and whatever our name was. We had to sew our name tags above the left breast pocket of our overalls. He told us that Corporal Smithers would be our father and mother for the duration of our training, and he too was on a first name basis: "Corporal!!!" We had not been given any specific course number yet, all that was to follow later. Boy, oh boy, there was a lot to take in, and not enough time to fit them in, but we soon got the hang of things. We were split up into groups of 10 and each group had to function. My group was on kitchen pool duty, which meant we had to report to the main dining room kitchen after parade and be instructed what our duty would be.

We assembled outside our barracks in a line of 3. We were marched to the mess hall for our breakfast. All our meals were buffet style. There was so much food, there was toast, bacon, hash browns, baked potatoes, boiled peas and carrots, baked beans, fried, boiled or poached eggs, and of course tea or coffee in big urns. We were seated according to our group, as we would be allocated a course number in the immediate future. I soon realised why they fed us so well.

After breakfast we were assembled back at our billets, marched to the parade ground. We stood to attention and waited and waited. After what seemed like an eternity we were told to stand at ease. It was a freezing open parade ground. We soon realised time was not of the essence, when we seemed to stand in queues for ages. We were taught fast, how to take our mark from the right, and turn left or right, about turn, halt, by the left quick march, left, right, left, right, mark time, etc. That was exhausting, and we did this for what seemed like hours. We did have the odd prankster, who would turn left when we were ordered to turn right. Most of us were new to doing drill, and we would burst out into laughter. He would be sorted out real smart, and so would we, as we would all have to do 20 push ups. We learned quickly that it was not a joke and things were taken seriously for minor infractions of discipline, and we all realised that we were here as a team, and all members were responsible for one another.

As it was almost time for our lunch, we had to march to the airman's' mess hall for lunch. Our lunch consisted of a buffet, where we collected our plates, cutlery, and tea/coffee mugs and there was an assortment of food in abundance. There was fried rice, white rice, assorted veggies, some baked and some boiled, mashed potatoes, and different kinds of sausages.

After lunch we assembled in our respective groups and waited for the DI to instruct us what we had to do. By this second day, we were forgetting to think for ourselves, as we were being instructed and shouted out continuously. We felt the pressure that the DI was going to be a major part of our lives for the next 12 weeks. As our recruit course, a course number, had not been allocated, we were put on pool duty. As I said before, we were divided into 3 lots of 10.

My group was taken back to the mess hall and reported to the SGT in charge who told us that we would be working on shifts, either breakfast, lunch or dinner. Our jobs entailed working in the kitchen, like peeling potatoes, carrots, onions or long beans, dicing beef, or sometimes cutting pork into cubes. We had gloves and hot water to clean the chickens and make sure there were no feathers. We prepared loaves of bread and margarine. We also had to set up tables that seated about 500 in long rows of tables and benches, seating about 50 airmen per row.

After the meals some of us were allocated to what was called "slop buckets and bins on wheels". We would clean the plates into the slop buckets and others would collect the cutlery and yet others would use damp cloths to clean the areas. We were busy "worker bees", and got this down to a fine art as it seemed like a constant flow of people filling the spots we had just cleaned. But we continued to work. After collecting plates, cutlery and cups, we would take them to the washrooms where there were industrial washing machines. Plates had to be put with plates, cups with cups and cutlery with cutlery and they would go through the machines.

There would be other pool duty boys at the other end and would pile all the plates up on trolleys, cutlery in their trolleys and the cups, for distribution into the mess halls in their respective places. This seemed like a never-ending line of hungry men. We would continue this work for a further hour after the mess was closed. After this we were allowed to have our meals, if we had not been able to have our meal prior to our shift. Then we would do the other jobs in preparation for the next meal.

The most challenging shift was the early morning breakfast shift, as we would have to report to the mess kitchen at 04:00 hours. We would start by checking that all tables, benches and the floor were dry, clean and tidy and all had to be ready in a timely manner for the breakfast at 06:00 hours. Making sure the urns for coffee and tea were boiling, the toasters were plugged in, and the assorted condiments like jam, honey, marmalade, marmite and butter/margarine were taken out of the industrial fridges and placed in the allocated positions at the head of the buffet area. Also, cold milk and hot milk were placed in urns and marked accordingly. There were a battery of cooks and each one knew his designated task. It was a sight to behold. Every aspect of the meal was taken very seriously, like boiled eggs, fried eggs, poached eggs, backed beans, assorted mixed fruits, prunes and small boxed assorted cereals, all ready for the impending assault on the mess hall by hungry airmen.

After a week or so of doing this mundane but important job, we were advised that the recruit course had an allocated number, and my course number was 1176.

I could not wait to start our training and looked forward to a more routine way on the parade ground and healthy physical training for the next 12 weeks.

After about 6 weeks of steady incremental training, both physical and classroom (where we learned military ranks, insignia, rules and regulations and military legal matters, and drill), we were beginning to look like a band of healthy young men and each day we were getting stronger, disciplined and a better cohesive team.

We were marched in formation to the armoury to get our rifles. The big day had come when we would get our SLR (self-loading rifles), which fired a 7.62 mm cartridge at a highspeed velocity. Then each of us were presented with our bayonet and a webbing belt with brass buckles. These had to be polished, so that our reflection of our face could been seen in it. Most of us had never set eyes on a rifle, leave alone fire one. The first thing we were taught was to respect our rifle and look after it as though our very lives depended on it.

We were taught to recite the following verse each day when we woke up. "This is my rifle, and this is my gun", holding our rifles up high and the other hand you know where … There were two ex-members of the marines from the British army, who taught us how to spit polish our boots each night. They had migrated to Australia on special visa, on condition they joined the Army, Navy or Air Force, so we were fortunate to get the benefit from their experiences. They were in their mid to late twenties. I was 23 and referred to by many as the grandpa. I was able to teach them how to make their beds with hospital corners, as was the usual method of making one's bed. I had learned how to make my bed that way in Dr Graham's Homes and had got used to doing my bed each morning, even at home.

Our first day on the rifle range was an experience that we had all been waiting for. After a couple of weeks of having it drilled into us by the DI how to assemble and disassemble our rifles and oil them and keep them clean as a whistle, and getting them inspected each day, it became second nature to us. We were marched to the firing range way down the other end of the airstrip and split into 3 sections. We were each given 30 rounds of ammunition and had to fill the 2 magazines. The excitement of being on the firing ground saw no bounds, as we were lying flat on our tummies and the SGT in charge of the range got us into firing position. Then he gave the order to fire and "bang!" Though I wasn't too sure where the bullet had landed, the casing had come out the side. We were then told to fire 4 rounds in quick successions, but after the second shot my rifle jammed. I did not know what to do and turned around to the SGT with the rifle pointing towards him. That was a lesson I was to learn, as he took one step closer to me and kicked the rifle out of my hands. I was petrified, then he explained that "You never point your weapon at anyone unless you planned to use it". I had to collect the empty casings and there were 3. He told me to remove the magazine and reload. I was then instructed to take a deep breath, hold it, and fire 2 rounds, which I did. I had found the target on 2 out of 5 rounds.

We were then ordered to fire 5 more rounds, and as we hugged the butt of our rifle into our shoulders, we were ordered to fire at quick succession on semi-automatic. The rounds came out in quick succession and by now had found the target, though the sound was deafening. After pausing for a while as we collected the spent casings and put them in our pockets, we were told to unload and remove the magazine and to reload the magazine that had 15 rounds. After getting into firing position, we would always keep an eye on the red flag on the top of the range, which meant that there was danger and live ammunition was being used. Then the order was given ready, fire in our own time at quick succession to the target. We took aim as best we could. Took a deep breath, held our breath and fired the remaining 15 bullets into the targets. We were getting the hang of things, and it felt great. We each had 5 more rounds to fire. After placing the rifle down on the ground, we then collected the other brass casings. We checked that we had 15. The last 5 rounds were great, as we were told to fire individual rounds at the targets.

At the conclusion of the weapon firing and retrieving the 30 casings, we had to produce our weapons for inspection to make sure that they were empty. Then we got a chance to retrieve our first ever range targets. I think to my recollection I managed to hit the target 17 out of 30 times and was quite chuffed with myself, though none were in the bullseye. After checking with others, I did not feel too bad as we were all about average, though the 2 ex-marines had high scores and a few bullseye shots. After handing in our spent casings to the armoury and signing the register, we were escorted off the firing range and returned to our barracks. That was one day I would never forget. Each week we would go to the range for target practice and slowly but surely got better and were filled with optimism and excitement, knowing that soon we would be marching out of 1RTU without the added title of recruit. There were a few more other tasks like physical obstacles and hurdles that we had to complete such as going for rout marches with a full pack: March 100 yards, then run a further 100 yards and so on till we had done 5 km. I was not as fit as I thought, but there was always another day. We had another 9 km rout march, and the day before our final passing out parade we completed our 12 km rout march. Though exhausted, we were relieved and knew we would soon be seeing our families.

Our last day had come. On 01 September 1972, we were going to pass out in full dress uniforms, with webbings and rifles all spit and polished.

The parade ground was prepared for us and all the drills, manoeuvrers, PT runs and marching were coming to an end. Our passing out parade was scheduled for 10:00 am and the base commander, unit commander and other VIPs and some family members were expected to attend. We did our thing as best we could and we must have done it well because our platoon commander and drill instructor said we had done a magnificent job and made them proud. Our last few days were hectic as we were going for our course training, some of us to RAAF Base, Wagga Wagga, NSW and some to RAAF Base, Point Cook to do radio, communication and data processing (computer). I forgot to mention that while I was on my recruit course, I was still getting paid from Austral Bronze Crane Copper PTY, as I was on official annual leave, and getting my RAAF pay directly into my account at home.

My first posting as an AC was to RAAF Base Wagga C&STS. I would do a further 12-week clerk course after which I would be allowed to go home for a week before joining my unit No2AD HQ, at RAAF Base Richmond NSW. During the weekends, we were allowed to leave Wagga Wagga for Sydney. On my first weekend, on Friday after lunch I managed to hitch a ride from a truck driver outside the RAAF base to Sydney. In those days there was a single lane highway and it would take us 10-12 hours, depending on traffic to travel to Sydney. I remembered coming home to Lewisham and must have arrived at nearly midnight, in full uniform. When I knocked on the front door, there to greet me was Theresa, who was carrying Ingrid in her arms. She was 14 months old with curly hair and she refused to come to me as she did not know who I was. I had a short visit and headed back to the base at 10:00 am via Liverpool where I hitched a ride with a truckie who was heading past RAAF Base Wagga Wagga. This commute continued for the three months, and by the time I got posted to RAAF Base Richmond it was early December 1972.

December 1973, I was promoted to LAC after I did my corporal promotion exam. I did not want to waste any time. I enjoyed my clerical duties and had good bosses to help me through this phase in my life. By now we had moved closer to RAAF Base Richmond at Bungaree Road, in Blacktown. I learned to drive and got my licence at Richmond on the first try, and purchased my first car, a dark grey Vauxhall Velox for $800. I taught Theresa how to drive and she too passed her driver's licence on the first go. We were quite settled, and life was good. Later in August 1974 we bought our first home at Rooty Hill for $24,950.

On Christmas Eve 1974, Darwin was struck by the category 5 Cyclone Tracey, which caused much damage and destruction. As soon as I heard this, I volunteered my services at RAAF Richmond, at the Air Movements section, as the RAAF was tasked with evacuating all women and children from the city, including many family members of the RAAF Base Darwin. It was horrendous as women and children were arriving in clothes they were in when the cyclone struck, and many were in a state of shock and traumatised by the experience. The record was broken by a Qantas 707 for carrying the most passengers ever attempted in the evacuation and the RAAF C-130 aircraft from 35 and 36 Squadron, and Caribous aircraft from 37 and 38 Squadron. I remember handing out boxes of sandwiches, fruits and blankets. I did eventually volunteer for the reconstruction program from March through to August 1975. I really enjoyed that experience, as I felt I was doing my bit for the people of Darwin and Australia.

While in Darwin, during the week I would work as a cleaner in the evenings in government offices, and other times loading shelves at Woolworths. I would also spend the weekends working as a labourer at the waterfront, loading bags of wheat, and other produce for export. We were paid well for each day's work. It was great, because at the end of my tour in Darwin, I had saved enough money to pay off one of our mortgages on our home.

While in Darwin on 30 April 1975, my niece Cecelia Cooke was born, and the South Vietnam military collapsed and was taken over by the North Vietnamese. There was a scramble to get as many Vietnamese people out as possible who had assisted America and her allies, including Australia, during the war effort. It was feared that there would be a massacre, and that started the escape by boat or any other means to sanctuary countries. In September I was attached to RAAFSTT to attend a course called No 28 CLKA Course from Clerk to Clerk Administrative. One of the criteria was the ability to type 60 words a minute. As I had completed a secretarial course in India and had jobs where I did a lot of typing, I found this a great refresher course.

In December 1975 I was posted to AMTDU (Air Movements Training & Development Unit), another unit on RAAF Base Richmond. Another challenging job, but I thoroughly enjoyed working in a joint Army and Air Force combined unit. At AMTDU I was a fully trained CLKA and of course, with each course completed a pay raise came along with it.

On the 01 April 1976 I was called in to Squadron Leader Dunn's office at about 10:00 am and he said, "you have been promoted to corporal, an NCO". I immediately thought it was an April Fool's joke!! He assured that I had been promoted and told me to sign my acceptance. I waited till after mid-day before I signed the document. That document that you signed said you were willing to be posted anywhere that the Australian Government required you. I signed on the dotted line, as that meant another pay raise. I enquired about sitting for my sergeant promotion examination, which I had been studying for. It covered discipline, procedures, military law and responsibility as a SNCO. I continued to do my duties to the best of my ability, and enjoyed my job. As I was promoted to CPL, it meant that I could be transferred wherever I was required in Australia.

Theresa now was working at Wyeth Pharmaceuticals in Parramatta. She would take Ingrid to Harris Park, where an elderly lady looked after Ingrid for a couple of years. In June 1978, I re-engaged in the RAAF for another 6 years and after a thorough medical examination was re-engaged till June 1984, and a $1,000 re-engagement bonus was given as an incentive, for the military was trying to retain members of the armed forces.

In November 1978 I was advised that I had been posted to Detachment A, a RAAF police unit in Neutral Bay, right on the harbour, and near the wharf where the ferries would come from Circular Quay. That was a great job, and I was responsible for all administrative duties. Again, another great posting, and I thoroughly enjoyed that posting. My boss was Squadron Leader Clarke, who was a fair and very supportive officer and left me to look after all the administrative duties without any interference. I was living in Rooty Hill and the driver of the unit lived in Mt Druitt. He would take a police car home each night as part of his duties, should he be required overnight, as the police worked 24/7. This enabled him to give me a lift to work – it all worked out fine for us.

By this time my grandmother and father had died, and my mother was looked after by my sister in India, and she had asked if I would try and sponsor her. She was finding it very difficult to manage. My boss encouraged me and supported my action by providing a supporting letter to the Minister for Immigration. My second child and first son, Graydon, was born in May 1979 at Blacktown Hospital after a difficult labour. We were advised that he would have to be delivered by emergency caesarean section. I was allowed to witness the delivery at 19:29 hours. We were overjoyed to welcome him into our lives as there was almost 8 years apart between Ingrid and him.

In October 1979, I was advised that I was being transferred/posted to RAAF Base Wagga Wagga, to Headquarters RSTT (RAAF School of Technical Training) on 04 January 1980. I was on Christmas holidays prior to my posting, and we were busy packing and getting ready for our move. I had organised for a married quarters and schooling for Ingrid in Wagga Wagga. On 27 December 1979, we had sold our above ground pool and got $40 for it. The gentleman paid the money in full, after dismantling the pool. About an hour later there was a knock on the door, and to our total surprise there was my mother! I was a bit perplexed as I had no idea she was arriving, and as usual the telegram arrived a week later. Anyway, we welcomed her and the taxi she had arrived from the airport in was out the front waiting to be paid. The bill was $40 and thank God we had sold the pool that morning for that amount. I had to rush down to Wagga Wagga the next day to try and change my married quarters as now instead of a 3-bedroom, I had to get a 4-bedroom. The RAAF had a policy that if you had a girl and boy in the family, they had to have their own bedroom, and now that mum had come, I had to organise a 4-bedroom MQ.

Our removal to Wagga Wagga was organised for early January 1980 and we were busy packing and getting ready for the removalist to come and clear our home. We had organised to rent our home while waiting for the quarters, though we were not too sure for how long. Theresa was not happy about leaving her home, but we had no option. It was a very difficult time for us. We moved to RAAF Base Wagga Wagga, and were advised that we would be staying in a motel with 2 rooms, which fortunately did not cost us anything. We were placed on the waiting list for married quarters. We stayed in this motel for nearly 6 weeks. Theresa was very unhappy, but I had my job and my duty to serve.

We eventually moved into the married quarters, a 4-bedroom home just opposite the Mt Austin Public School. We booked Ingrid into the school, and Theresa managed to get a job in the kitchen of the Wagga Base

Hospital. As we now had mum with us, she was a great help, looking after the children for us.

I worked very hard in the new department looking after the apprentice documents and their examination results. I loved the job as a corporal and settled in well.

On 01 June 1980, I was summoned to HQ and informed by the commanding officer that I had been promoted to the rank of sergeant. I was thrilled to bits as this gave me more responsibilities and another pay raise. I discovered that my promotion had surpassed about 80 more senior CLKAs, and that it had taken me almost 8 years to obtain the rank of SGT where the average was 12 years. I felt "I must have been doing something good". I knew that I loved my job and that reflected on my determination to do well in my career. Before I signed the document, I said a prayer and thanked God for his providing and seeing us through the last 8 years. After signing the promotion document, I was congratulated by the CO and my joy was beyond words. When I got back to my office, I was advised that I would be transferred within the base to another section called C&STS as an instructor, training young members of the service as clerks (CKLs), and clerk administrative (CLKAs). I had completed a Sergeant Supervisory and Management Course, which equipped me to perform my duties as an SNCO. This course also equipped me in training and management of the members, just out of recruit training, and their new roles in the RAAF.

I applied for leave and decided to take my wife and children to Perth. My mother was not keen on coming and she was happy to stay home. My neighbours offered to look after her, as the area we stayed in was mainly occupied by members of the RAAF and their families.

It was the first week of June, and we decided we needed a break from all the stress involved in our moving and the upheaval during the last 6 months. We took off for the more than 4,000 km trip to Perth, across the Nullarbor Plain from South Australia to Western Australia, a dead straight road for 400 km. It was on this road that we could hear the clinking sound of coins and discovered that Graydon our one-year-old was having fun and happily throwing out all the coins from the console through the window. Luckily for us, the last clink sound, which were our house keys, got our attention and that was when we decided to check it out. We stopped the car and proceeded to find our keys and coins in the middle of the road. We salvaged what we could and proceeded.

We got into Perth after almost 4 days and nights of driving. We brought our tent on the roof of the car. We would pull over to the side of the road and pitch our tent and pump up the airbeds. After dinner, we would lie down gazing at the stars and finally drop off to sleep. I would get up at about 4:00 am and pack the tent and put the kids in the car and we drove off. After 4 hours later and we'd covered some 400 km we stopped and had our breakfast and wandered around as we took in the breathless and beautiful sights of the wilderness of the desert, in the centre of Australia. Our trip to Perth gave Theresa the opportunity to reunite with her mother and catch up on lost time. This also enabled her to visit some of her long-lost cousins, uncles and aunties.

Theresa's mother (Mary Elliot) had always lived with Theresa's cousins (the Elliot family) as a caregiver to one of their wheelchair-bound disabled daughters. When the family migrated to Perth, they brought her along with them. Mary Elliot had a difficult life both in India and eventually in Australia. Till her last breath, when she died of cancer, she faithfully lived with the family, rendering her services. She was buried in an unmarked grave. When we visited Perth again, after her death, Theresa and I made a proper and fitting headstone with a proper marbled gravesite, as a tribute for her. This was the least we could do, and we felt good paying our respects to her.

On return from leave in July 1980, I was transferred again, within the base, to C&STS as an instructor teaching CLK and CLKA courses. I loved this experience. My first experience was under the supervision of FSGT Brian Sela, and co-instructor SGT Russo. I completed my first 10-week course in September. I thoroughly enjoyed the experience and looked forward to instructing my first course, 100 CLK. I was surprised as this course consisted of 7 girls. It was a great experience and I always referred to them as "my girls". I took some of them out one weekend at the end of the course to meet my wife and kids. After a sumptuous Indian meal that Theresa had cooked, we headed to the skating rink in the middle of town. My first experience skating. We had good fun as I crashed many times to everyone's delight. I conducted a few more courses of CLK and CLKA in 1980-1981. Then I was advised I had been posted to HQOC.

HQOC (HQ Operation Command). This headquarters was for purely operational aspects of the RAAF, mainly flying and operational bases. This was based in Penrith, on big grounds between the Council Chambers and a new shopping centre. This posting was great, and I enjoyed working in the orderly room in the movements section. The new HQOC base was being constructed at the foothills of the Blue Mountains at Glenbrook. It was early 1982 that we moved into the new buildings, which was very well planned and convenient for all of us. In the new building, I was in charge of the Registry. There was a side office called the S&C Registry where all correspondence would come to us via telexes and messages and mail. My team and I would collect all the mail as it arrived, and then allocate it to the respective staff officer that needed to action the file. We were one of two big HQs, the other one was in Melbourne called HQSC (Head Quarters Support Command). This Headquarters was responsible for all training and support services, like, spare parts, stores depots, training and other aspects of support. All control of the two commands was co-ordinated through the Air Force Command and Department of Defence situated in Canberra (the Australian capital). The Minister of Defence was the civilian boss, and the chain of command flowed through him to the CDF (Chief of the Defence Force), then on to respective heads of the Army, Navy or Airforce, and each of their Headquarters, either operational or support. I worked here for 5 years and in 1984, re-engaged for a further 6 years of service and another re-engagement bounty, gladly received and paid directly to my mortgage.

ACR - R. A. Cooke – August 1972 with my new SLR.

ACR – R.A. Cooke Pass out Parade – 01.09.1972.

RAAF 1RTU Course 1176 Pass Out Parade -01.09.1972.

RAAF No: 57 CLK Course – September 1972.

RAAF - LAC R.A. Cooke with daughter Ingrid – 1974.

RAAF – CPL R. A. Cooke promoted 01.04.1976 – AMTDU.

RAAF No: 28 CLKA Course 1980.

RAAF No:30 CLKA Course – 1981

RAAF No:100 CLK Course – "My Girls".

RAAF SGT R.A. Cooke promoted 01.06.1980.

CHAPTER 12

A family in crisis

On the morning of 4 October 1983, it was our 14th wedding anniversary. It was a beautiful warm spring day and I had decided to wear shorts and long socks. I was contemplating either taking our children to the beach or a drive to RAAF Richmond base for a picnic.

I walked around the lounge room and my daughter Ingrid noticed that the sock on my right leg had slipped down to my ankle. She called out in an urgent way, "Dad, look at your sock on the right leg". When I looked down, she was correct, and I noticed the calf muscle had wasted away and the sock was at my ankle.

In the last six months when in RAAF Base Darwin, while involved in Exercise Pitch Black we were in a tropical uniform which consisted of short-sleeved shirts and shorts with long socks. I did not notice anything wrong with my right leg. Both Theresa and I were anxious that something must be wrong. We decided to get it checked at the Mt Druitt Hospital, A&E department. After a brief wait, we were called by the doctor who asked me general questions about my health. I said, "I am a member of the RAAF and completed a full medical examination a couple of months ago. I am due to re-engage for a further 6 years starting in June 1984 and passed the medical with flying colours." He then asked, "When did you first notice this muscle wasting?" I told him, "My daughter had noticed this, only this morning". After a lot of prodding and checking my reflexes with the little hammer that doctors used when checking reflexes, he said,

"There is a decrease of activity in your right leg". He continued with the strength tests for my arms and other leg. I noticed the doctors in the emergency room looking quite concerned. They were talking among themselves. I heard the term "atrophy". Both Theresa and I were alarmed as the difference between both legs was a good 2 inches difference in circumference. I was asked to report to 3 RAAF Hospital for further investigation with a neurologist.

I was transferred to No 3 RAAF Hospital, Richmond NSW, and was put under the care of Dr John Corbett, a neurologist. After a thorough examination and checking of my wasted calf muscle, he then ordered that I be admitted to the Concord Repatriation Hospital for a battery of tests.

A lumbar myelogram with a dye was conducted. I was placed in a flat position on the bed with strict instructions not to move under any circumstances for 24 hours and after that to stay in a sitting position for another 24 hours.

I was then subjected to an electric shock all over my body. It felt very uncomfortable as the needles were put in my arms, then my legs and all over my body. Then an electric current was applied to measure the reactions of my neurons in my limbs and body and a series of back and chest X-Rays were taken. After a week, I was told, "Stay home for 2 days before reporting for duty at HQOC".

After a week or so of waiting on 01 November 1983, the day of reckoning had arrived. I was driven back to Dr John Corbet for a diagnosis and prognosis. I was invited into Dr Corbet's consultation room. He said, "The results have come back and confirmed my suspicions". The tests have confirmed you have amyotrophic lateral sclerosis (a type of motor neurone disease), a serious neurological disorder". I was shocked, as I had no symptoms apart from slight weakness in my right leg and getting fasciculations (twitches) all over my body recently. Dr Corbett, in his calm and soothing way, informed me, "You will be in a wheelchair within 6 months, and death will follow in two to five years".

That was a shock to take in as I was still a young and fit man of 37 years old. I was in the prime of my life. I looked at him and simultaneously said, "Wow, I am lucky". He looked at me and said, "How can you be lucky, when I have given you a death sentence?" Without batting an eye. I said, "You have given me 2 years. I could leave your office now and get hit by a bus.

At least you have given me 2 years where I can plan the future for my wife, who is 34 years old, and my 2 children; my daughter Ingrid is 12 years old, and my son Graydon is 5 years old".

I had accepted my fate without going through the grieving process. It so happened that Dr Corbet was about my age. He assured me, "I will be there to manage your medical situation as your condition progresses". I had a lot of questions but as I was in a state of shock, I was not able to ask further questions. He said, "Wait in the waiting room while I notify your medical officer at HQOC". After that, Doctor Corbet shook my hand and said, "I will see in a month's time".

That was my longest trip home as I was weighing all the pros and cons on the best way to break this news to my wife and two young children. I came to the conclusion that the only way was to be honest with my diagnosis and prognosis. Theresa knew from the look on my face that the news was bad. I asked my mum, "Can you please keep an eye on the kids?" I then said to Theresa, "Since 04 October 1984, you have watched me going for all those tests. Well, I have the answer. I have been diagnosed with amyotrophic lateral sclerosis, also called MND". She asked me, "What do you mean?" I replied, "It is a rare neurological disease, and according to the specialist I will be in a wheelchair within 2 years and be dead in 5 years". We hugged each other and cried our hearts out and tried to console each other that all would be fine. Though we knew deep down this was very serious, we both felt we needed to take one day at a time whatever lay ahead us. We promised each other that we would be honest with the children and my mother as they had a right to know, even though it really broke our hearts.

We came out of the room and sat mum and the children down. I proceeded to tell them the truth. I said, "Dad has just come back from the specialist, and he has told me that I have a serious illness called ALS or MND, and we have to be strong, and look after each other." I asked, "Is there any questions?" There was dead silence. No one responded. I told them, "We love you very much, and we will get through this together as a family".

As you can imagine, there was silence and shock then eventually tears came flowing down, as we all did a group hug and were determined to get through it together as a family. Hence the term, "A Family in Crisis".

We slowly got back to our daily lives. I tried to find support services in the telephone book. There was not much information or support services in those days. The internet was being developed for military purposes and instant communication only. I then decided to do my own research and discovered that amyotrophic lateral sclerosis was a form of motor neurone disease. ALS for short was a term commonly used in the USA and Canada and European countries. The Americans also called ALS Lou Gehrig's disease, which was all too confusing. I was determined to find out as much as possible

It was then that I approached some OGB schoolmates in London, England, as I had heard that the actor David Niven died in July 1983 at the age of 73. He was a well-known accomplished actor and Academy Award winner. After his death the family helped raise awareness of MND and was instrumental in raising about 700,000 British pounds for scientific research, welfare and education, as well as for the provision of medical support staff, for example, physiotherapists, occupational therapists, speech therapists and nutritionists. There was a big need for medical equipment to assist in the day-to-day management of ALS/MND sufferers.

I was grateful to receive much information from the MND Association of the United Kingdom to help me understand what was before me.

I was still a member of the RAAF, and I continued my normal work, though I was getting progressively weaker in my legs and getting cramps in my hands and my feet as well as my muscles were twitching all over my body. If I could explain it, I would say it was like there was a mouse running under my skin, down my back, and on my limbs. It was a weird sensation. I continued to receive much support and encouragement from the principal medical officer of the RAAF, Group Captain Graham Killer, who continued to monitor my progress on a regular basis and took a keen interest in my welfare, for which I will be eternally grateful. There was much to come, as I grappled with and juggled my daily family life.

Family in Crisis June 1984.

CHAPTER 13

My RAAF comrades' gift of friendship

Time was ticking away and in December 1983, I had gone for my usual medical check-up with my neurologist for a morning appointment. Unknown to me there was a surprise waiting for me at the SNCO's mess at HQOC. The SNCO's mess was patronised by senior non-commissioned officers and I being a sergeant in rank and a member would go there for a meal at a subsidised rate. There was a bar, as is customary in any military establishment, formal dining at nights and of course we were able to address each other on a first-name basis. Above all there was that camaraderie and friendship.

On return from my medical appointment, I was summoned to the SGT's mess and was advised that the members had an extraordinary meeting and had contributed for me and my family to go for a 10-day fully paid holiday, wherever I wished to go. I was totally blown away by their kindness and generosity. When I returned home and broke the news to my wife she immediately said, "No Ray, you must go and take the time to enjoy this holiday that was provided for you during your hour of need by your service mates".

I felt it was a wonderful gesture from my comrades. I did fly to Auckland, New Zealand and it was a wonderful trip, as I was able to catch up with quite a few OGBs in Auckland. I met with Tauten Kesang and his wife Gwen and two girls Tshering and Elizabeth who took me to their home for dinner. It was great catching up after so many years apart. But one thing fabulous with us OGBs is no matter what your status or station in life, when we meet up it is as though we had just left yesterday; it is a unique phenomenon. I also caught up with Nancy Webber (Halliday) and her boys Christopher and Johnathon. From Auckland our coach took us for an overnight trip to Rotorua, a beautiful resort filled with the smell of sulphur, from the active volcanic boiling hot water from the ground. It was here I was to experience the Hangi or native Mauri feast. After some more sightseeing we headed back to Auckland for the flight to "windy" Wellington the capitol. After a day of further sightseeing and enjoying the views including the "beehive" or parliament building, it was here later in the evening that I met my old school friend, George Borthwick and we had a good time. After burning the midnight oil, I went back to the hotel. The next morning, we were going to cross the straights between the North and South Island. Something that took my breath away, there were hundreds of dolphins racing alongside the ferry. The ferry ride took us to Picton on the South Island of New Zealand. After staying overnight in our hotel, our coach headed down the west coast. We headed south to Fox Glacier. We headed on to Arrowtown where the bungie jump was invented. I watched this in awe, a daredevil experience. With only a of couple of thick rubber bands tied to each of his or her feet, one then jumped. This seemed like an eternity as the screams of the person pierced the air and they almost touched the beautiful jade coloured, fast flowing river. The colour of the water, as explained by our tour guide, was caused by the oxygen trapped in the glacier, by the ice compacting, crushing, moving and melting. I was not game to try this adventure as the coach driver was trying his best to entice anyone of us to volunteer. I had learned from my Air Force experience never to volunteer. After this fabulous experience, it was on to Milford Sound. As we rounded the corner, the sight of Mitre Peak was a magnificent view to behold, the beauty of God's creation.

The following morning, we viewed the snow-capped mountains called the Remarkable from the hotel dining room. We took in the beauty as we had our breakfast. On a cruise in Milford Sound, I watched the waterfalls and mountains on each side. From there we drove along the South Island to reach the typical Scottish countryside of the southern hemisphere, to a city called Dunedin. A beautiful city with magnificent buildings, one of which was the Dunedin Railway Station. The city had a lot of open spaces, gardens, parks and green hills, which reminded me so much of my youth, growing up in the foothills of the Himalayas. It was here I was able to catch up with another school and classmate of mine from Dr Graham's Homes. Her name was Lorraine Law (Rogers) and her husband Roy, and their two children Steven and Anita. After another round of sightseeing organised by the tour, Roy and Lorraine collected me from the hotel for an OGB get together, with a potluck dinner and a great singalong. What happy memories, with another bunch of OGBs as we sang the night away with old favourites from our school days. The end of the trip was drawing to an end. As our coach drove along the Canterbury Plains in Otago, we were able to see Mt Cook. After much excitement and some more photographs, we arrived in Christchurch. We had reached our destination. After some sightseeing and visiting the Christchurch Cathedral, we headed off to our hotel for the night. The next morning, we flew back to Sydney. I returned home to my wife Theresa and the children, who could not wait to see what goodies I had got them. It was great to be home. The photographs say it all.

Family reunion on return from NZ-February 1984

My return from my trip to NZ – February1984

Theresa all smiles on my return from NZ – February 1984.

CHAPTER 14

Our worst fear

Willis Street in Rooty Hill, where we had purchased our first home, was an ideal location close to the railway station for both Theresa and I to go to work. The home was purchased through the recommendation of a work college of Theresa's at Wyeth Pharmaceuticals at Harris Park. Since we lived near the railway station, it was convenient for Theresa to take Ingrid to the babysitter in Parramatta and was a 5- to 10-minute brisk walk to work. Our home in Rooty Hill sat on a fair-sized block of 760 square metres. One would be lucky to get a concrete driveway for that price these days, yet even after many renovations it was not up to scratch for wheelchair access.

We decided to sell our home and build another home with more manageable measures for mobility needs, as my disease progressed. I was encouraged by my neurologist to look at doing this before my condition progressed or deteriorated to the wheelchair stage. We saw similar advice from the literature we were reading about other more practical mobility issues.

After much discussion and planning, we found a vacant block of land at the end of a tiny cul-de-sac right on Willis Street. I enquired with my neighbour who owned the land and he offered to sell the block of land for $34,000. I needed to find someone who could build a good practical home, suitable for my requirements and special needs.

We found a good builder, who we knew because he had done the renovations to our old home. He promised us that for a round figure of $50,000 he could provide all landscaping, fencing, driveway and, of course wheelchair access.

We were excited to see our dream come true each day as we drove past the new home being built. We put our present home on the market as the new home was nearly fully constructed. We sold our old home for twice the amount that we originally paid.

One blessing was that my neighbour who sold the land to us had known us for the last ten years. He found out about my condition and when he heard that it would cost a further $6,000 to construct our home over the easement for pier and bearing, he graciously waived that cost. So, we got the land for $28,000. We were so grateful to God for his provision again for us. We moved into our new home on 23 March 1984, a date that I would never forget, but that story later.

I would like to share some anecdotal information. As the new block of land was just some 100 meters from my existing home, I realised I would not have to move too far, and the children could be in the same school with their friends. The block of land had some large trees which needed to be cleared, if I was to construct the home that would fit comfortably. I searched around for someone to help remove the trees, and got 3 people to give me a quote. When the first person came to quote, I walked from my home to the block to show him the trees. I was not too strong on my feet at that time, and the first quote was $450 to cut down, remove and clear, I said I would get back to him. The second person's quote was $400, to which I gave the same answer. By the time the third person came to quote, I was beginning to get tired with all the walking. Anyway, we walked to the block. He offered to do it for me at $350. By this time, I was so exhausted, I stumbled and just fell. He did not know my medical condition and thought I had "fainted" with the shock of his quote. Low and behold he immediately cut it back to $300 and got the job. We both had a good laugh when I explained to him that I was tired, and my leg had given way. That was the end to a magic day!

Our new home was built, and was suitable for wheelchair access, as my prognosis had indicated. We moved in on 23 March 1984.

Theresa had a slight persistent cough, and as time passed it progressively got worse. We did see our GP, who thought it might have been an allergy or a cold, as it was coming into the flu season. We did not think much of it. I remembered on Graydon's fifth birthday, we took mum with us and celebrated his birthday at the Pizza Hut in Mt Druitt as a family. We did take some family photographs and later took a family portrait of the four of us in a studio. We purchased a photographic deal called "Magic Moments" and at that time it was very expensive, but we were able to capture some truly magic moments. That photograph from June 1984 was the last photograph we had taken as a family.

CHAPTER 15

A medical dairy in chronological order of Theresa Philomena Cooke

On Wednesday 11 July 1984:
Theresa had a severe coughing fit and after that she called out to me from the bathroom, and there in the sink was fresh blood that she had coughed up. We rang up the afterhours doctor, a Dr I.C. Pragnal, who attended and reported his findings to our GP Dr Castelino on Flushcombe Road, Blacktown. Dr Castelino ordered an X-Ray, and after the X-Ray we took it back to our doctor. She informed us that she thought it important, that we see a chest specialist Dr Ian Gardener and take the X-Ray for him to examine. We were booked in to see him urgently, and he fit us in on Friday 13 July 1984.

Friday 13 July 1984:
Dr Gardener ordered a further series of tests, another chest X-Ray, and a cat scan and Theresa was admitted to Westmead Hospital for further tests under Dr Ian Gardner in Ward 5A.

20 July 1984:
A biopsy was ordered by Dr MW Jones from the department of radiology.
23 July 1984:

A whole-body scan was conducted and further tests.

30 July 1984:

Dr. Bradstock of the haematology department advised me that Theresa had a large cell non-Hodgkin lymphoma. He got down to business and laid it out for me. He said she had a massive tumour in her chest. He told me she had a 50% chance of a cure, by having a massive form of chemotherapy called MEDCUP, consisting of 6 different chemicals. Dr Bradstock advised that he was referring Theresa to Dr Jerry Koutts, who advised us he would be taking over Theresa's care and treatment.

1 August 1984:

Commenced day one of chemotherapy, which consisted of a program of 5 treatments, of which day 1 and 2 would involve large intravenous infusions and course of tablets. For day 1 and 2 she would remain in hospital and day 3-8 return home. As Theresa was experiencing nausea, she was prescribed stomatal along with all the other tablets she had to take.

8 August 1984 to 29 November 1984:

Back to hospital in the oncology ward under the care of nursing staff who look after the chemotherapy and their patients in Ward 5A. The chemotherapy regime continued, and it got more difficult as the days went by.

I was fortunate that my bosses at HQOC were very kind and supported and assisted in so many practical ways, especially the days I would have to take Theresa to the hospital for her treatments. For the first couple of days of each treatment she would be admitted to the hospital, and my bosses were very flexible and allowed me to come in to work later during the day.

I really appreciated the support but would make every effort to continue my work. At times, I would be working till late into the night to catch up on my workload. I did not want to appear to be taking advantage of our dire situation, so I always made every effort to continue to do my job. As I had mum at home, she was a great help to me, by taking care of the 2 children.

We persevered and continued with the treatments, and each one made her feel worse. At the beginning, she started losing her hair gradually and as the treatment continued, by the time of our 15th wedding anniversary, she had lost all her hair. We were able to get a wig and turban from the Cancer

Council. Theresa found the wig difficult to cope with as she felt it was too hot, but each person tackles their situation differently. She continued her third and fourth treatment.

On the 22 November, Theresa's condition was gradually getting more difficult to manage and she started getting ulcers in her mouth and throat, and she began having difficulty swallowing food unless it was pureed into thick soups.

29 November was the commencement of the fifth treatment and Dr Koutts had decided for Theresa to start radiation treatment, under Professor Langford. We were scheduled to meet him on 10 December along with Dr Koutts at the radiation department at 15:15 hours. On 17 December they commenced simulation and marking for the radiation. She commenced radiation treatment on 22 December 1984 each day through to 3 January 1985. After 10 treatments, I remembered taking Ingrid and Graydon to see, encourage and wave to their mum on a few occasions during her treatment of chemotherapy and radiation. As difficult as it was, we felt that they had a right to know what was happening to their mum. The radiation was scheduled for 6:30 pm each evening, to enable me to attend my workday. I was quite surprised it would only take a few minutes, then we would be on our way home. There was no Christmas or New Year breaks for the radiation department. They worked 365 days a year, and the staff were so dedicated and kind in the difficult job they did. They are true angels.

3 January 1985 was the last radiation treatment and simulation, after which we headed home.

8 January 1985:
Dr Koutts rang and advised us he wished to see us urgently and made a time to see us the next day. He had some bad news for us and said that the simulation had shown secondary tumours at the base of her neck on the left side, another tumour was in her right lung, and one near the heart. But the most disturbing was that the tumour in her chest had returned and appeared at the original size. He further informed us that there is only one option left and that is to do a total bone marrow replacement, under general anaesthetic, followed by a massive dose of chemotherapy over 3 days, followed by blood transfusions and then pump back the treated bone

marrow. There was only a 30% of success, and her survival was now in the order of 2 months. He asked us, "Think about it, and get back to me". We had a literal life-and-death decision to make. I left the decision with Theresa and promised her I would support whatever she had decided. She told me, "I have suffered so much for the last 6 months, and I have only 30% chance of success". She then said, "I will continue with the radiation till 30 January 1985". Dr Koutts understood our decision and offered to be there should we need him at any time. He told us, "Try and take a holiday as soon as possible and spend some quality time together as a family". He gave us his personal contact no and told us, "You could ring me at any time you need me".

5 February 1984:

We took up the offer of a holiday home that the RAAF owned at Coffs Harbour. We booked for 5 nights at a nominal fee, and drove up there with Ingrid and Graydon. Theresa always loved the beach, which reminded her of her younger days at Paradeep Beach in Orissa near Cuttack in India. We had a wonderful holiday, as the kids enjoyed the beach and Theresa would sit near the rocks and do tape recordings for each of the children. She asked me, "Please present these recordings to the children on their 21st birthday or when you feel the time appropriate". I promised her, "I will do whatever you ask". Then joking she said, "Whatever you do, don't die before me". Both of us had a death sentence on our heads. Doing that act of love must have been excruciating, but she wanted to do it. We had resigned ourselves to our fate and were in the Lord's hands.

Theresa's condition gradually got worse on our return to Sydney. She had started having difficulty in breathing and got to the stage where she required oxygen. Dr Castellano, our GP, organised the oxygen and a palliative care nurse, Jill Sullivan, to visit Theresa each day to make sure she was comfortable. We just took one day at a time, and tried to make life as normal as possible, under these difficult circumstances.

18 March 1985:

Dr Koutts rang to find out how she was. He had been in touch with the palliative care nurse and understood from her that Theresa had a temperature and was having trouble in breathing despite being on oxygen. He advised us, "Contact your GP and get her to admit Theresa to Mt Druitt

Hospital, and I will advise the hospital of her current situation". He then said, "Because of her breathing difficulties, I think she may have developed pneumonia". I contacted our GP and related Dr Koutts's instruction. She then organised the admission for Theresa the next day.

19 March 1985:

Our GP organised for an ambulance nice and early to take Theresa to the Mount Druitt Hospital, with an update of her condition. I followed in my car. She was admitted and placed in a room by herself. The following day I rang and spoke to Theresa. She told me, "I had a good sleep but was getting a bit of pain. I am being annoyed by a fly in my room. Can you bring a fly swat?" I dutifully did what she asked me to do and brought the fly swat. That evening she rang and in an excited voice said, "I managed to get the stupid fly".

There was a steady stream of visitors at the hospital to visit her. Father Grady came and gave Theresa the last rites. Theresa was starting to get tired. Her childhood friend Joy Gail would love to visit her and kept her company, staying beyond the visiting hours as Theresa would ask her to stay with her and not to leave. She would hide from the nurse's station near the ward, and at times she would sit on the floor. I remember the first time I met Joy was when we were staying in Palace Street in a one-bedroom flat, a short while after we got married. Joy had just arrived from India. They continued to chat and catchup with their past experiences in CKP, and as it was getting quite late, Theresa asked Joy to stay the night. Unknown to me this had already been discussed that I would sleep on the floor in a sleeping bag which I did not mind as they were long-lost friends. I was always happy and obliged with Theresa, as she with me, in our relationship. We had mutual respect and a truly wonderful and loving relationship.

Theresa's last meal at the hospital was prepared by Joy. She had cooked hot pepper water and rice for her, which Theresa thoroughly enjoyed. Joy had known Theresa as a child and they had grown up with each other and especially enjoyed their time together at railway colony at CKP, which, if my memory serves me right, was a hub of activity for the Bengal Nagpur Railway. Joy's father was a mail driver and they lived in the railway quarters close to where Theresa lived with her Granny Sutton, whom she loved dearly and cared for.

On 22 March 1985:

Dr Tan from the hospital rang me and advised me, "Come now and see your wife with the children to say your farewells." We rushed over to see her at 6 pm. After about 30 minutes she was getting restless and tired. It was a very emotional time. The children were crying and upset, and I was coping with my own emotion. We held her hand, kissed her and said our final goodbyes. Theresa responded by waving to us as we left, and I looked back at her for the last time.

I do remember it was a clear sky, star-filled night and as we were leaving, I looked up and showed Graydon the sky and told him to choose a star and that would be his mum, if mum should die. That was the last time we saw her alive. The next morning on 23 March 1985, the phone rang at 6 am, it was the nurse in charge of the palliative care ward. She informed me that Theresa had passed away peacefully at about 4:00 am. When I went to the hospital, the doctor said, "I was with Theresa when she passed away peacefully without any pain or fear. She did not want to disturb you or the children and asked me not to ring you before 6 am".

She was a loving and considerate wife right to her last breath. I took the children to her for the last time. As we walked into the room, we saw the curtain was drawn around her. We stepped in to see her. It broke my heart to see my children crying out for their mother as they saw her lying still on the bed.

I do remember that Yvonne and Brian Vanjour, whom Theresa knew in CKP in India, and we became close friends, came to assist me to make the memorial cards for the funeral service. We looked after their 2 boys who were babies when we lived in Blacktown.

We had discussed and prepaid the funeral arrangements We had also purchased a family plot of at the Kemp Creek Catholic Garden Cemetery. The funeral was organised for 10 am on 26 February 1985. The service was held at St Albian's Catholic Church. Father Grady conducted the service. Many children from St Aiden's Primary School (Graydon's school) and St Agnes High School (Ingrid's school) attended the service. It was a simple but beautiful service. We went to the cemetery after the church service and suddenly the sky opened and the rain came down in buckets. As the coffin was lowered into the grave, Graydon investigated the grave, filling up with water. He turned toward me and asked, "Dad will mum get wet?" I hugged him and reassured him, "All will be well. Mum will be okay". As the raining continued, we scattered.

Raymond, Theresa and Family from 1980 – 1985.

Theresa and the children at Coffs Harbour NSW – February 1985

Theresa Philomina Cooke- Memorial Card -23.03.1985.

CHAPTER 16

A new chapter in my life

We had to get our lives back in some order, as we returned to our normal day-to-day activities. I thought about my work at HQOC. I knew my career was coming to an end in the Air Force, as I had been reclassified to remain in the Sydney area, close to medical facilities and my specialist. That would unfortunately put me in a position that I would not be promoted, due to the limitation of posting availabilities. I was advised that I would be discharged MUFD (medically unfit for further duty). That had a big impact on me, as I had signed on for my third re-engagement of six years, taking me up to 20 June 1990. I needed to get my affairs in order and prepare for an early retirement.

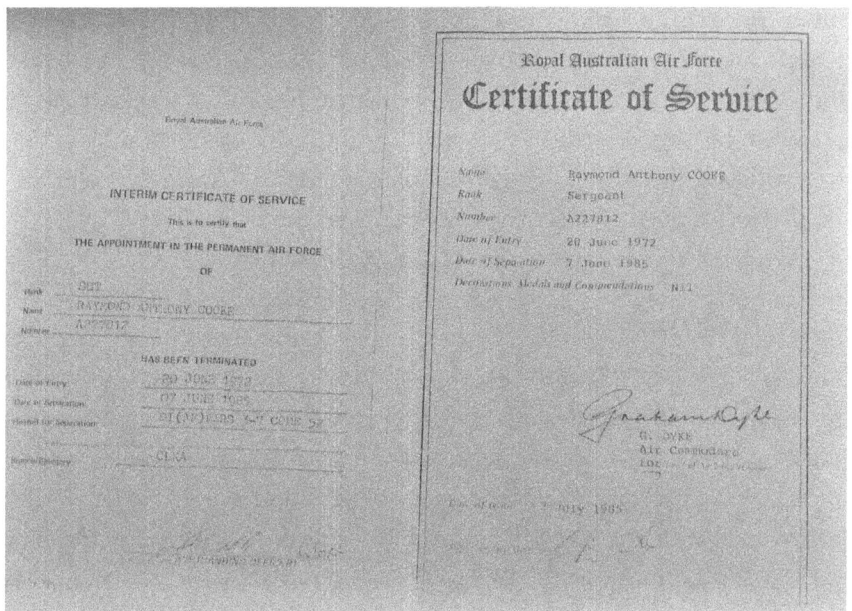

Certificate of RAAF Service-07.06.1985.

There is one story that I must share with you. Throughout my RAAF career, somehow whenever I arrived at a unit one of my responsibilities was the running of the tea club. That would entail purchasing, providing and procuring the supplies for the morning and afternoon tea/coffee breaks. The most important item was the financial side of the deal, when the supplies and stocks, were running low. Each payday on a fortnightly basis, I would collect $2 from each person in my unit or area of responsibility.

I would collect the funds and purchase the tea of coffee in bulk, which is needed when one was in a big unit, such as the HQOC HQ or main office. There were close to 300 personnel, and it was my duty to provide the best service, to boost the morale. I always had a bit of fun, as I approached each person from the unit no matter what rank, from air vice marshal down to the LAC (leading aircraftman or private). This duty was "serious business", as I had to account for every dollar spent.

I would then go to the local bulk buying outlets to purchase the necessary supplies for the month, as it was always good to have a ready supply. I would always purchase the most expensive coffee and tea for the first purchase. Gradually, over time, I would replace the contents of the expensive containers with cheaper brands. This sleight of hand enabled me to purchase biscuits and other goodies for when we had welcoming rituals for new members transferred in, or for those being transferred out. We would also procure cakes and finger food on a regular basis to celebrate birthdays, additions to families, and even marriages. It was on these occasions that I would approach the new member, welcome them, and finally advise them of the fortnightly financial contribution of $2.

On my retirement from the RAAF, I had to hand over the "baton" to the new sergeant who would take my place.

It was then that I disclosed my secret purchasing powers, and the tricks I used to keep each one at the HQ happy. I was really surprised, and so were the recipients of my largesse, that they had never even suspected that the top-class coffee/tea that they were accustomed to be the cheapest, no-name brand on the market. One of the senior officers asked me, "How and why, were you able to pull this off?" to which I replied, "Didn't you notice how during the last four-and-a-half years, there was always biscuits and cakes during the morning and afternoon tea breaks, and the cakes and finger food for celebrating special events?" Those who were present burst out laughing. That was my secret mission and people could not believe their eyes. They had come across the best "snake oil salesman" in the RAAF. They all appreciated the joke, and we parted as best friends.

My biggest concern was my financial position, once I had been discharged from the RAAF on medical grounds. I still had my two young children and an ageing mother to consider in any decision I would have to make. The children's schooling and their future welfare were paramount in my mind. I had to do what was best for them. They continued with their studies, ballroom dancing and other after school activities. Mum was there helping to take care of the children as and when needed. This was a great help!

My involvement with the ALS Society of Australia took on a new meaning for me. I decided to take up further responsibilities on the management side of the organization. I was still keen to see the formation of a specific MND Society of NSW, bringing us in line with the other states, and subsequently forming a federal body to assist in the huge projects of research and public awareness. I joined with other likeminded sufferers in the hope that we would one day see a national Motor Neurone Disease Association of Australia. This would require getting neurologists to see my point of view, and the intended consequences of the national body. This dream became a reality. Another thing to tick off my bucket to-do list.

I joined the Lions Club branch at Rooty Hill. We would meet each month for dinner meetings and discussions of future plans for fundraising for our local community, projects and other pressing needs. One of the good things that the Lions Club of Australia did was raising funds for MND sufferers, who required aids for mobility and their daily lives. I took on the role of coordinating with other chapters of the club in Australia as the equipment officer of the MND Association of NSW. This entailed visiting clients and assessing their needs, as and when we saw them evolve, as they would change, sometimes rapidly, depending on each situation.

I found this work very gratifying, and it gave me much encouragement. I could see from what we were doing with our limited resources that we were able to benefit so many people and their families to come to terms with this terrible disease. I was so busy with all that needed doing that I did not have much time to dwell on my own predicament.

In late 1987 I approach a group of friends and the Leonard family of Clontarf, NSW for fundraising. Lady Leonard lost her husband Sir Walter Leanord, to this dreadful disease and she and the family, who had lost a loving husband and father, were determined to give all their support. They were determined to support me 100% and proceeded to help me raise much-needed funds for research and equipment for sufferers, as well as awareness because MND was not very well known or understood. We decided to hold a black-tie ball at the Sydney Town Hall.

This was a challenge. I had to put in many hours of preparation for this event. I required a lot of support from friends and family to keep my children engaged, as they were young and very energetic. After many months of meetings and hard work, eventually everything came together for the event. In late 1987, the Ball was held, and it raised a massive amount of much needed funds. "Phew!" $28,000 in one night was indeed a great shot in the arm.

The Lions Clubs of Australia had a special project to raise funds toward awareness, and the purchase of much -needed equipment as well. I would drive over many distances all over NSW, talking to groups of patients and the people who cared for them and their wellbeing. At the same time, it was a steep learning curve for me, and I put all my administrative experience into the formation of the MND Society of NSW.

I had been attending a small church in Sevens Hills, called the Emanual International Christian Fellowship. It was through this Christian group I got a lot of spiritual support and a new lease in life. I started to get more involved in church life and made a lot of friends, who are still good friends to this day. Many of these friends had known me for the last 30 years, and we now attend the Castle Hill Baptist Church, on Showground Road, Castle Hill.

CHAPTER 17

The turnaround of my life in an upward direction

In 1989, I was still actively involved in my work in the MND Society of NSW and The Lions Club. I was fortunate enough to have appeared on many radio programs. I was very fortunate to have done a 10-minute television segment on the promotion of the work in research and equipment for MND on Channel Ten's *Good Morning Australia*.

One of my church members in the Emanual International Christian Church, Mr and Mrs Raj, who were from Singapore, decided to introduce me to a friend of theirs. Both knew of my situation as a widower with two young children. It was through them that I was invited to attend a good old Australian bar-b-que hosted by Barry and Ester Gracie in Baulkham Hills on 5 May 1989. I discovered that Barry had been a member of RAAF and was at AMTDU (Air Movements Training and Development Unit, which was a joint RAAF and Army unit), doing a course in relation to his work when I was there in 1975-78. He was a loadmaster and was a Vietnam veteran. It was at their place and at this meeting that I set eyes on my future wife Evelyn, and it was "love at first sight!!" After which I was a frequent visitor to their place.

Her father had arrived from Singapore, along with her 2 sisters, brother and sister-in-law, nieces and nephew.

After discovering her dad originally came from Calcutta, and had migrated to Singapore as a young man, I proceeded to try and charm him with my language skills. I recited one of the famous Bengali poems by the well-known poet Sri Rabindra Nath Tagore, "Ama Dey Chota Nodi, Chole Ake Barke….". which I had learned in school. Evelyn's dad was multilingual, so I thought I would try to impress him. He turned around and spoke to his son in Tamil "Poi karan, nabathe", and everyone burst into laughter. It was much later that I discovered what he said, "He is a con. Don't trust". He must have picked up that I was trying to impress him. Being a retired police officer, his instinct must have interfered with his judgement. After lunch we went to Parramatta Shopping Centre, and it was there that we discussed the prospect of marriage with her brother. Also being a police officer, he grilled me for almost 2 hours. He asked me, "What is your working background and why do you want to marry my sister?" I replied, "I had studied in India and migrated here to better myself. I was in the RAAF and was medically discharged. I was married once and my wife had died five years ago, and I have 2 children, aged 10 and 17". I was forthright about my medical condition and financial status. I promised him "I will look after your sister".

We kept talking and I discovered she came from a large family of 7 girls and 2 brothers, and that he and his dad had been very protective of the girls. He told me, "Dad brought us children up after our mother died when we were all very young and dad never remarried". The more I learned, the more I appreciated Evelyn. The family returned to Singapore.

We started meeting and going out frequently. Over time we got to know and understand each other. We would attend church together, and at times she would visit with me and met my two children. I felt very comfortable with her, and on 14 February 1989 I took her to the Rooty Hill RSL Club for a dinner. It was Valentine's Day and a soft romantic song "Where Do I Begin" by Andy Williams from *Love Story* was being played by the pianist at the corner of the room. We got up and danced. When we returned to the seat, I popped the question "Will you marry me?" She looked at me and said "Yes". Then I took the engagement ring and said, "I want us to be engaged before you leave for Singapore". I slipped the ring on her finger. We agreed that we would get married in October and that I come to Singapore to marry her, as most of her family and friends were there.

Unknown to me, she had approached a good school friend of mine, Lorraine Law (Rodgers), and invited her to the wedding. It was all a big secret. As we prepared for the big day, I left most of the preparation to Evelyn. I said to her, "You organise and let me know and I will fly down to Singapore for the big day". A date was set. When Evelyn rang and asked, "Will the fourth of October be a good date for our wedding?" my heart skipped a beat. This date, unknown to Evelyn, was a special date all through my life in India and again in Australia. These were the events that took place:

(1) My good school friend George Borthwick's birthday
(2) I left Dr Grahams' Homes, Kalimpong in 1960
(3) I left St Thomas Boys' School in 1963 and finally
(4) Theresa and I got married in 1969

I was quiet on my end of the phone, not being able to say anything. She took it as "Yes" and went ahead to organise. She rang the next day and told me, "The place for the reception was not available on that date. Will it be okay for the second of October"? I was relieved and told her, "That date would be a great date. It is Mahatma Gandhi's birthday". In the meantime, I had completed all the paperwork to sponsor her to join me in Australia after we were married.

Unknown to Evelyn after she left for Singapore, I wanted to surprise her and had grown a beard for the last 3-4 months after her departure. I sent a picture of me with my beard to her brother, who had the same weird sense of humour as me. I decided to purchase a box of mangos to take with me to Singapore. We arrived about a week before our wedding as there were still a few things that needed to be sorted out. Both Graydon and I flew down to Singapore. My mother and Ingrid stayed home, as she had her studies to attend to. I arrived in Singapore, and all the family were at the airport to greet us. I walked out of Customs with a box of mangos on my head and of course with my beard. Her brother burst out laughing and I could not help laughing either "ha!" as I saw Evelyn's expression. She could not believe her eyes. I could see her eyes wide open in shock.

Evelyn had her 4-room apartment, and it was very spacious and comfortable. It was then that unknown to me that Lorraine Law had arrived, and I was really shocked and almost collapsed when she showed up at the door. It was indeed great to have someone in my corner, especially as she was my old school friend from DGH in Kalimpong, India.

The night before our marriage, Evelyn's brother Tom was able to get a special bungalow where we could have the reception after the wedding. With the help of Lorraine, Graydon, her 2 sisters, the nieces and nephews, we decorated the place for the wedding next day.

Tom had a friend who loaned us a car and we decorated it with ribbons and bows that Evelyn's oldest sister had done for the wedding. We were collected and driven to the Registry of Marriages. At about 2 pm, we were ushered into the hall with a big, long table. At the end of the table was the magistrate, and Evelyn and her dad were opposite to Lorraine and me. Her dad was the witness and so was Lorraine, beside me.

The wedding ceremony got underway and after signing the papers, the magistrate turned to me and asked, "Where are the rings?" I started to shuffle into my pockets, pretending I did not have them and had forgotten to bring them. Of course, Tom was aware of the trick and so was Lorraine. It was planned for Lorraine to hold the rings and delay handing them over when asked. Evelyn was shocked and the magistrate was impatient. I turned to Lorraine, who slowly pulled the rings from her bag and handed them to me, struggling to hold back her laughter. I said to the magistrate, "Oh there they are." The "boss" and the magistrate were not too impressed. Tom was videotaping the whole process. We did have a good laugh, after the exchange of rings and we were pronounced as husband and wife.

After the wedding ceremony, Brother Tom had organised for us to spend some time in the Singapore Botanical Gardens taking pictures and videos. I was in a woollen suite. Can you imagine being in the tropics with a woollen suite!!! I must have lost about 5 kg after 2 hours.

We changed into our formal attire for the reception. Evelyn had a beautiful gold and red-bordered sari, and I had my Air Force dress uniform. The reception was at the bungalow in Pasir Ris, near Changi airport. Evelyn had organised a buffet dinner/banquet, catered by Singapore Airlines Catering Services. Being on staff at the airport, she had her contacts. The food was absolutely beautiful. Ingrid did ring us from Sydney to congratulate us, which was really nice.

Evelyn had organised for us to visit Fraser's Hill, a famous resort in Malaysia where many people went to get away from the heat. We left Singapore after a couple of days, after registering the wedding with the Australian Embassy in Singapore, lodging some documents and making an appointment to see an Australian immigration official on our return from Malaysia.

After we cleaned and tidied up the bungalow at Pasir Ris, we headed off to the border crossing at Woodlands. We were in a large 12-seater van and had to dismount and proceed through immigration and customs, which took a couple of hours and long queues. After walking through to the other side, we got our passports stamped, boarded the van and headed off towards Kuala Lumpur, the capital of Malaysia.

We finally drove up to Fraser's Hill. It was a single road and traffic headed in a single-file convoy, all the way to the top. Once we moved into our respective bungalow, owned by the Singapore Government and leased out to government department employees, we went on a sightseeing tour. Evelyn's nephew Peter was a confident and expert driver. He navigated the winding road to the top of the Fraser's Hill safely. It was a beautiful, cool and a relaxing climate.

Graydon enjoyed himself with his new extended family. There was an old lady called Pati who took a liking to him. She showered him with kisses whenever she saw him, which I am sure he remembers even today. He was 10 years old, and she called him, "Valakara payan" which means "the white boy".

We then travelled to Tanjong Malim in Malaysia, where Evelyn's niece Lydia, her husband Jones, and two children made us feel so welcomed and comfortable. I remembered Lydia making a Malaysian special dish called sambal Tumis, a beautiful spicy side dish with shrimps, chillies and "blachan" (shrimp paste). One had to get used to the smell of "blachan", it was delicious and something to remember. I tasted the durian, an exotic fruit, for the first time and nearly felt sick. It had a pungent smell which lasts for ages. This is banned in all public transport in Singapore.

On our return from our trip, the next day we went to the Australian High Commission for an interview and final granting of a visa for Evelyn to enter Australia, on marriage ground. The immigration officer spoke to us, "I have received the marriage certificate, what will you do if I did not give permission for your wife to join you?" to which I replied, "Simple, I will stay in Singapore, as long as it takes". She was taken aback by my quick response. She disappeared and returned shortly and said, "You have been granted the visa to return to Australia with your new wife".

We returned to Australia after three weeks and settled down to our newly married life. We visited Barry and Ester in Baulkham Hills on a regular basis. I took Evelyn to meet my mother, who was now residing at Our Lady of Consolation Home in Rooty Hill. Evelyn resumed her work at the BHRS (Baulkham Heights Residential Services). She had worked here before our marriage on a voluntary basis, and enjoyed the job, so she returned there on a full-time basis. After nearly five years, she started work at Westmead Hospital, on our wedding anniversary, on 2 October 1995, first at the University Clinic and then at Women's Health, where she retired in August 2015 after a wonderful and fulfilling career, and a well-earned retirement.

Framed Studio Wedding Photograph 02.10.1990 – Singapore.

Roy and Lorraine Law (Rodgers) My School friend who came for my wedding from NZ to surprise me.

CHAPTER 18

Our special friends Edward and Jeba Martin for the last 31 years

On 9 December 1990, we attended the Christmas Carol service on The Hill at Rooty Hill. It was there that Rev Drake from Rooty Hill Uniting Church introduced us to an Indian couple, Edward and Jeba Martin. They had 2 children, Emanuel and Priya, who were schooling at the time. Edward was a history teacher at Blacktown Girls High School and his wife Jeba worked in the Australian Tax Office. We chatted for a while then Edward asked us, "Would you like to join us at Rooty Hill Uniting Church?"

I have never asked my friend if he has ever thought he made one of the biggest mistakes by asking me to join his church.

Both Eve and I enjoyed going to the RHUC at the Rooty Hill Public School Hall, where the church service was conducted while the new church was being built. It was almost at the final stages of construction. We had many happy memories there and made some lifelong friends between 1990 and 2005.

I would love to share some happy times we had there. First and foremost, it was a very cosmopolitan congregation. There were very talented musicians and singers. Over a period of time, our numbers grew, and our congregation was a "close-knit" family. Edward and Jeba, who were the first people to invite us to this church, came from Tamil Nadu in South India and spoke Tamil, which my wife could speak too, having been born and bred in Singapore and of Indian descent. One of my services to church, that I had inherited on a temporary basis, which lasted for nearly 10 years, was publishing and printing the weekly newsletter. We had many wonderful occasions. We would have progressive dinners, which was a fundraising event at a nominal fee of $5 per head or maximum of $20 per family. This event would start at 5 pm at one home with finger food, followed by another home for the main course, and from there to the next home for sweets and desserts. Finally, the last home would provide coffee, tea and a light supper. This would come to an end at about 11 pm. A lot of work went into these events, and we all had such good fun.

On one occasion, we went for a men's retreat by bus to an undisclosed destination. We usually took a sleeping bag and did all the cooking for the weekend. By the time we got to our destination it was getting quite late. As we were nearing our destination, we could see the accommodations were cottages and dormitories with a big hall for the cooking and preparation of meals. We pulled into the driveway and as soon as the doors opened, it was every man for himself.

I thought that I had I found the ideal cottage. I rushed into one of the cottages, straight into the bedroom where there were bunk beds, and placed my sleeping bag on the lower bunk. The top bunk was occupied by Trevor, a big man and an old miner, who has migrated from Wales. By the time my friend Edward had dismounted from the bus there was only one room in the dormitory. He asked me, "Ray, you are my friend, how come you did not reserve a bed for me?" I told him, "Bad luck, you were taking too long to get off the bus, first come, first served", with a chuckle. In the middle of the night, I was awoken by the snoring of Trevor in the top bunk. It sounded like an express train had come crashing through the front door. All night I stayed awake listening to his snoring. I regretted rushing to choose this cottage.

The next day I said to Edward, "You can have my bed if you want" to which he replied, "Serves you right for rushing to get the best bed in the house". Edward was aware of Trevor's snoring as everyone was talking about it at breakfast. It was probably my old school instinct, when growing up as a child one had to fend for themselves. To this day he has never forgotten that experience. We laugh and talk about it.

Another occasion was my friend Edward's 50th birthday, and it happened to be on a Sunday. We were at church, and it was my turn to do the announcements. I went up to the front of the congregation and said, "Let us all wish Edward a happy 60th Birthday". Edward was shocked and tried to protest, but the rest of the congregation believed me. My poor buddy Edward, what he had to put up with. Our friendship continued to grow stronger over the years. He was a glutton for punishment.

We have travelled around Australia and to many parts of the world. One of these special moments was when we travelled to Egypt and Israel together with a tour group. Unknown to Edward and Jeba, we were going to Fort Lauderdale for their son's wedding after this trip.

In Egypt we had great fun time on the Nile cruise and then to Cairo. At the hotel in Cairo almost toward the end of our tour, Eve had gone shopping with some girlfriends, and I stayed behind in the hotel on the 20th floor. The view was awesome. I stepped out onto the balcony and closed the glass door to keep the air in. After checking the streets and bridges below, I tried to re-enter the room. To my nightmare, the door was shut. I tried all means to get back in but wasn't able to. I was panicking and looked over the balcony and saw a couple of policemen. They were guarding the front entrance of the hotel. Frantically, I tried to draw their attention, but they kept waving and shouting something back. It was hard to hear each other as I was on the 20th floor. I could see their gesture and faintly hear "stay". It was the longest 5-10 minutes until 2 security men appeared in my room to open the sliding door. They had been given to understand that I was a potential jumper. I explained "I was locked out", to which one of them asked, "Did you not know there is a small button at the bottom of the door that releases the lock?" I replied, "No, I did not see it". We had a good laugh at my expense. I gave each of them US$5 and they were very happy. When we were checking out, my travel companions could not believe that I was being treated like a VIP and getting saluted by one and all the police officers on duty. It turned out the US$5 I had given as a thank you was the reason for the special treatment.

We headed off to the airport and caught our connecting flight to Israel. Israel was a truly wonderful experience for us and as Christians had a special significance. After our 10-day tour we bid farewell to Edward and Jeba as they we heading to the USA via London to attend their son Emmanuel and Jessica's wedding in Fort Lauderdale, in Florida.

We headed the opposite direction via Japan. After an exhausting trip to Tokyo our connecting flight to LAX airport was held up for 6 hours because of engine trouble. After waiting at the airport for what seemed like an eternity, we were given a food voucher of 6,000 yen each. We could only buy a hamburger at McDonald's with the voucher, so we bought a burger each; that was the end of our meal vouchers.

We were on a tight timeline for our flight to LA in the US, owing to the 6-hour delay. When we reached LA we had to rush through immigration and customs, and we had only 30 minutes to dash to the other end of the LAX airport. We arrived just as they closed the boarding gates. One of the ground staff was very helpful and saw our plight. She managed to book us on another flight via Atlanta to Miami. We settled into our flight and eventually arrived at our destination after a good 28 hours of flying. We landed and there was a message waiting for us from the bride's parents, Mike and Karen, who were to pick us from the airport. After waiting for hours, they decided to go home, so we took a cab to the hotel. Both Mike and Karen knew that our arrival at the wedding was a surprise for Edward and Jeba.

The next morning, nice and early, we caught a cab to their home in Fort Lauderdale, I had my video camera all ready for the big surprise, and we saw our friends heading towards us. They were happy to see us but were laughing their heads off. The evening before, not knowing how we were getting to their place, Karen asked, "who is collecting Ray and Evelyn?" Edward heard and so the surprise was squashed. After all the hassle with our flights, we were excited to share in the happy occasion, the wedding.

After the wedding, we went on a 7-night Caribbean cruise to end our first trip to the USA. On our way home, we headed off to Las Vegas and the Grand Canyon, the Hoover Dam and on to San Francisco for a few days before heading home. That was a memorable holiday of a lifetime. All organised by our friendly travel consultant Eugene from Flight Travels at Blacktown.

By now we had really got the travel bug and used Singapore as our base for future travels to Japan, China, Vietnam, Thailand, Malaysia, Cambodia, Sri Lanka, and China again.

Our next trip to India via Hong Kong and New Delhi was another experience we would love to share. This time our trip to India was to visit and surprise our dear friends Edward and Jeba. This time all went perfect to plan as we had their son Emmanuel and daughter-in-law Jessica with us.

Emmanuel, their son, had made all the arrangements for the trip and our secret surprise. Incidentally, Jeba has a mean sense of humour. I discovered that she and I shared the same birthday 29th December, though not too sure about the year.

We went on a roundabout way to India via Guangzhou in Southern China, where we tasted all the delicious food of Canton in China. From there we headed to Hong Kong by train. It was a wonderful trip.

On our arrival we had another surprise for Emmanuel's friend James as it was his 50th birthday. It was all organised by Jessica for us to meet him at a dinner. He had no idea we were coming to make his big day a special event. The restaurant was high up on the Hong Kong Harbour with a panoramic view. After the big surprise we then told James we were coming along with him to New Delhi in India then to Chennai. This was his first visit to India. We arrived in Delhi and to James's horror, he panicked when he saw how precariously his luggage was tied to the top of the van. We finally got to our hotel. Emmanuel, his wife Jessica and son Aaron, and James were going to do the Rajasthan Triangle. Eve and I stayed in a guest house near the Karabagh Markets for a few days so that we could take in the sights of New Delhi. After Emmanuel and family and James had completed their Rajasthan experience, we caught our respective flights and arrived at our destination in Madurai, the resort that Emmanuel had booked for us to stay. Both Jeba and Edward were staying at the same resort, unaware we were there. Lunch was organised for everyone to meet at the dining room. Edward and Jeba had their backs to us by design as we sneaked into the dining room and just stood behind them. Emmanuel pretended to take a picture and said, "Dad and mum turnaround!" Oh boy! That was the biggest surprise for them as they jumped up screaming with elation of joy. They were so excited that Edward went around telling everyone in the dining area about our surprise visit. This trip really made up for the disappointment of our intended surprise for them for the wedding in the US.

From there we headed to Madurai, Jeba's birthplace in South India. After a bit of sightseeing and shopping, we headed further south till we came to Ramanathapuram. I had heard so much about this seaside town in South India, which is the nearest point between India and Sri Lanka, Palk Strait. After all the years of friendship and discussions with Edward and Jeba, at last we were going to meet his large extended family and shared in their generosity and hospitality. That was one of the highlights of our lives, and our friendship for each of our families blossomed from there even further.

Another of our trips was a 23-day cruise from Durbin to Venice with our travel companion Danny and his wife Vivien Ng. After a long trip from Sydney to Abu Dhabi we were waiting at the airport to catch a connecting flight to Durbin. We turned to see the queue, and who should we see, Jeba and Edward also catching the same flight to Durbin. That was a real payback for the Indian surprise trip we did. So just to give you an idea we have made many friends over the last 30 years through our travels, but our friends Edward and Jeba have always been there through good and bad times.

Edward and Jeba Evelyn & Raymond.

Emmanuel and Priya, the children of Edward and Jeba, always saw us as their parents too.

Edward and Jeba

CHAPTER 19

Moving into our retirement home 5 May 2005

We decided to purchase and build our retirement home in a new suburb in the Baulkham Hills Shire Council in Northwest Sydney. This was to be, hopefully, our final home to retire and live our remaining years in harmony and tranquillity. The suburb was a new estate called Beaumont Hills, between Kellyville and Rouse Hill, and was a paradise for open spaces and a new, family-friendly environment. We bought a block of land and built our dream home through Eden Brea Homes. It had been decided that we would construct a single-storey home with a small backyard and garden and by all accounts it had to be a maintenance-free home.

My wife Evelyn took on the role of "construction manager" with a passion I had not seen in her before. She took on the role of interior decorator and all the colour schemes were her choice, especially the kitchen, as she loved her cooking and baking. The smell of freshly baked cakes wafted through the home and would be a welcome sign for any visitor, whether friend or family.

As we were deciding to sell and move, we had a lot of apprehension as we were moving to a brand-new area, new neighbours and friends, and above all from our comfort zone at Rooty Hill as I had lived in that suburb since 1974 (30 years). For me this was a gigantic move, but it would be our last. We hoped that God would guide us in this big milestone in our lives.

We had been attending the Rooty Hill Uniting Church over the years, and we had built up a reservoir of great memories and friends. Our farewell from RHUC was a great event and we were truly humbled by the number of friends that attended and their warmth that was bestowed upon us. We did finally sell our home and coincidently the settlement all took place on the same date as we got the keys to the new home.

We were busy looking for a church and we felt that God had brought us to the Castle Hill Baptist Church. On the first Sunday, this young lady introduced herself to us and welcomed us. Her name was Eunice Wu, she was from Taiwan, and became a good family friend. She was just 27 years old at that time, treated us with respect, and above all made us feel welcome to the new church. Over time and sharing many Indian dinners, we got to meet her parents and her future husband Ted. We were invited to their wedding on 11.11.2012 at Hunter's Hill on a beautiful sunny day and for the reception at a function hall overlooking the harbour. Today they have a son called Albert, so we have christened them as "TEA Family" (Ted, Eunice and Albert). We have remained as good friends for the last 16 years, and now as she has her own family, we always made it a point, prior to the pandemic and lockdown, to go out for a meal and fellowship at least two or three times each year, and to celebrate special occasions together.

We were also fortunate to have met friends, that we had met many years ago from our previous church, these friends had known me before I had met and married Evelyn. Denis and Luci Low, encouraged me to write this book, among others like Rocky, Savvy and their two girls, Zenia and Savvy. In fact, it was Rocky that painted Mt Kangchenjunga for me. That gave me the inspiration to tell my story. We still attend the church and have been involved in the church activities and made many good friends there at CHBC. Our lives were blessed by our reunion with our old church friends, and we have been involved in a bible study group, and other church activities. Later that year I celebrated my 60th birthday, and we had a home full of family, friends and OGBs to celebrate together. It was truly a blessing, and great way to celebrate our new home.

The area was slowly being developed and our neighbours moved into the area. We just happened to be the first occupants in our neck of the woods. God has blessed us with a wonderful group of neighbours and friends, and over the years we have seen their children grow up. The Rouse Hill Town

Centre was opened in 2004 with just a few stores, like Woolworths and Coles and the banks in between. We saw the centre become a hive of activity with residential dwellings and apartments, more shops and eventually after a couple of years there was a Medical Centre, with doctors, dentists, pathology, a library, physiotherapist and radiology. There were parks and walkways being developed, with modern playgrounds for children with all the accessories springing up all over the area. One of the highlights is the New Metro railway link to Chatswood, with construction and plans for the line to be extended all the way to Bankstown and the new airport at Bargery's Creek. We are happy in our new surroundings and getting comfortable. We thank God in our daily walk with Him. We felt that God had planned our future and was guiding and blessing us each day.

Eunice on her birthday on 06.09.2005.

Evelyn and Eunice 09.01.2007.

Ted and Eunice wedding day 11.11.2012.

The Ted, Eunice and Albert "TEA" family.

Zenia, Rocky, Tania and Savvy Family.

Denis Low and Dr Lucia Low (Bong).

Rocky Starr, my friend, inspiration and above all an artist.

Special painting of Mt Kangchenjunga by Rocky Starr

CHAPTER 20

Visit to my first home Dr Graham's Homes, Kalimpong, WB India 12-17 October 2012

On 12 October 2012 we flew to Bagdogra airport, where our transport was waiting for us. Our driver Pradeep was an experienced driver and knew all the roads like the back of his hands. I was so excited that I even offered to sit in the front of the jeep near the driver. There were many close shaves on the road with trucks and other drivers; even though it was a two-lane highway, it was still very narrow. It took my breath away as I saw the Coronation Bridge leading toward the eastern part of India that lay beyond Bangladesh and toward the Brahmaputra River. The best silt-filled plains for crops of rice and other produce, and in the hills of Assam were the tea gardens that would produce tea. During the time of the British, tea was exported all over the world. The other parts of India that grew tea ware Darjeeling and the Nilgiris Hills in South India.

As we were driving, I began to practise the little Nepali that I was able to speak, interlaced with Hindi, though he spoke fluent English. At least we were able to communicate. I felt happy that at last I was coming back to my old school after an absence of almost 52 years to the day I left on 4 October 1960. My arrival in Kalimpong, as we drove the winding road along the side of the Teesta River, was fascinating as the memories came flooding back. Finally, after almost three-and-a-half hours we came across the new Teesta

River bridge, as the old one had been washed away after a major landslide upstream and subsequent flood that created much havoc and loss of life.

Before we left Australia, we had organised to stay in Kalimpong, at the Orchid Retreat Ganesh guest house, with transport at our disposal. Our hosts Ganesh and his wife, and daughter-in-law Honey, warmly greeted us on our arrival. It was getting late and since we had travelled since early morning, we decided to call it a day, but our hosts insisted that we have our dinner before she showed us to our room, that overlooked the plains of India that we had just left. After a beautiful home-cooked meal, we headed to our room, and after a good refreshing shower, we called it a night as we had a few busy days visiting my childhood home.

After a hearty breakfast our driver was waiting for us, to take us to the school compound on 13 October 2012. As we approached the main gate, my heart skipped a beat as I was returning to the first 15 years of my life. It was nice and early and just before assembly. The chapel and other buildings had sustained quite a lot of damage after a severe earthquake that had struck the area a year or so earlier. We were fortunate that I was able to meet the headmistress Mrs Peacock. She was kind and gracious to me and after advising her I was an OGB we had a brief discussion, she introduced me to those who were present there and welcomed me to go wherever I wanted to go on the compound.

I immediately felt at home and went to visit the Lucia King (the infants and babies' cottage) and we were met by the superintendent. She showed us around and I remembered that I was in the blue section, and all our beds, dining tables, play areas were either blue or pink. I assumed blue for boys and pink for girls. We went out to the play area, and there were 20 or 30 children with the nurses. The children were spontaneous and when we asked, "Would you all like to sing a song for us?" Without hesitation, they burst into the song, "Ring and Talk to Jesus" with actions. It was so beautiful, and my heart filled with nostalgia as that could have been me 67 years ago. After being shown around the playrooms and witnessing the destruction from the earthquake, fortunately it was not too serious. The plaster had fallen off the walls and this was in the process of being repaired. After that we drove past the flower hot houses, the swimming pool, and followed the road past Elliott Bend where in my time I would buy snacks from the boxwallah. From there we continued up toward the school building and noticed that the clock tower was half the size as it had been damaged some time back by an earthquake. We passed the kindergarten, Jarvie Hall, school classroom blocks, the headmaster's office, the science block and veered to our right and there was my old home "Calcutta Cottage". We met the houseparents who were kind enough to show us around the cottage, the kitchen, dining room, toilets and wash/shower room. I noticed that all the sports shoes were lined up, this was something new, as in my time we never wore shoes, even when we were in our Sunday best (in this way we were treated as equals, and shoes were not in our wardrobe). All the timber floors were well-polished. As it was in our day, one would use a wax polish and we would have polishing rags tied to our feet and we would run up and down to get the floors to a high sheen. After this we climbed up the stairs, which looked a lot smaller than I had imagined them to be, well-polished with a wooden banister. Directly in front of the staircase were a few toilets, on my right was the small boys' dormitory, about 15 beds lined the walls and all the beds were made, and towels neatly placed at the foot of the bed. I immediately noticed a boy near the window, and he was sitting on my bed. I indicated to him, "that was my bed when I was in Calcutta Cottage". He was a bit shy but very polite, and he asked me "How many years ago?" I told him "I was there from 1950-1960". We then crossed over to the big boys' dormitory, and this too was spick and span. We then headed down to the sitting room and had a cup of tea and snacks with the houseparents.

Next, we visited the Kathrine Memorial Chapel, which had suffered some structural damage from the earthquake. We were able to proceed with caution. I remembered how much time we had spent there each morning in reflection, before our school day would begin. I had attended Sunday Service as a child here and it still looked wonderful, and the three stained-glass windows looked more beautiful as the sun was shining and the light coming through. It came back to me how as a child I loved to attend church and with over 500 children and staff in their Sunday best, we sang many beautiful hymns that I had never forgotten. It was one of the highlights of the week. Many of us had learned to sing in parts and in unison, and to this day it is still a wonderful experience.

We continued our way up to the Steele Memorial Hospital, where I had been admitted many times with my frequent asthma attacks and after the serious one that put me in a coma for 5 days. I remained in the hospital and attended school and my classes, as arrangements were being made for me to be transferred to the plains, at St Thomas Boys' School in Calcutta (Kolkata).

The next day we visited the cemetery where Daddy and Mrs Graham were buried exactly 23 years apart to the day (Kathrine Graham died 14 February 1919 and Dr Graham died 14 February 1942). Then we visited the hospital, taking in the sights of Kalimpong. From this vantage point we were able to view many of the boys' cottages and girls' cottages, divided by the school classroom blocks and playground. We then proceeded to the bakery, stores, clothing department and the farm, with the cattle, sheep, pigs, chickens and also a fish farm. After all this excitement and after all those years it felt as though it was just yesterday that I had been here; all my childhood memories came flooding back to me.

Our driver Pradeep then drove us up to the highest point that is Dalo Hill to try and view Mt Kangchenjunga. We were fortunate that it was a clear day, and we were able to absorb the beauty of the Himalaya Mountains. As the majesty of the mountains came into view, I thanked God for bringing me back to my childhood experience, and how as a child I would love to sit and gaze out for hours, especially from October through to April each year. I would love to try and get there at sunrise and sunset to view the changes in colour from purple to orange and bright gold. It was just so magnificent that we were fortunate enough to have experienced these scenes freely given to us.

After lunch and purchasing some local trinkets and handicraft, we headed back to our holiday home at the Orchid Retreat back in Kalimpong. The next day we had organised with the help of Honey to visit Darjeeling, again that was a wonderful experience as we stopped along the way to take photographs and take in the views of the Teesta Valley below. As we got closer to Darjeeling, we witnessed the tea gardens spread along large swathes of fertile land, and the workers busy plucking leaves and placing them in a basket on their backs. It was fascinating to watch this work taking place, as a majority of the workers were ladies of Nepali and Lepcha background. They had done this work over the centuries, when the British were in India and continuing after independence. We arrived in Darjeeling and again our host Honey found a quiet little tea house and the view from the huge glass window displayed the majesty of Mt Kangchenjunga. After sightseeing and shopping we returned to our guest house. It took us another hour or so to drive back to Kalimpong.

One of the main reasons for our visit was the Toy Train, of which we missed out. We were given to understand that this ride was quite popular, and we should have organised the tickets before we came to visit. The Toy Train chugged up all the way from Siliguri up to nearly 7,000 feet to its destination at Ghoom Station, the highest railway station in the world. It was wonderful to listen to the chug, chug, chug as the train headed to the station in Darjeeling, though it did not travel at a high speed. People would run at the side of the train as it chugged all the way up the hill.

The next day we were going to attend the Sunday church service at Dr Graham's Homes. It was being held at the Jarvie Hall, as the chapel was under repair. It was great to see each of the cottages attending in order, the girls on the right and the boys on the left. Eve and I were up on the balcony as I wanted to record the service in full. I was so happy to have the opportunity to attend the service and as usual the singing was always a highlight of the service as the children sang with gusto, in unison and again singing in parts and that made it all the more memorable. After the service we were introduced to many of the staff and teachers, and some of the elder students.

The next day I got permission to go to the main office, so that I could see my history. I cited my arrival and some correspondence from my father with the school, asking about our welfare, and that was when I discovered the file of my mother and Aunty Alice, which was most revealing. Again, a good opportunity to try and gather as much information on my family as I could.

We said our goodbyes and farewells to all who made our stay such a wonderful experience. On the last day, 17 October 2012, after a hearty breakfast we said farewell to our wonderful hosts for the week we stayed there. Our driver Pradeep took us back down the mountains to Bagdogra Airport, to catch our flight to Calcutta then to Howrah Station. As we waited on the busy platform in Howrah Station, we noticed the railway attendant dragging something along the platform, where people spit their red pan juice. Little did we know but that was our bedding for the overnight sleeping compartment. Eve was struck dumb when she realised, we were the recipients of this first-class bedding. We made this trip to Hyderabad to catch up with my sister Judy, her husband and 4 boys. We were there for only 2 days. I had not seen my sister or her 4 sons since Calcutta in the early 1960s. Her boys loved cricket and sports. We made the effort to take them to the shops and market to get whatever they needed, since who knows when I would see them again. Though it was short, it was again great to catch up with members of my family and try and fill in the blanks. To connect us for the night train trip to Hyderabad in Andra Pradesh, we missed our train stop, but fortunately the next stop was not too far away on the other side of Hyderabad. We finally got off and our transport driver realised we had not got off at the correct stop and proceeded to the next station. We were indeed relieved to have had a good driver. All these arrangements had been taken care of by our faithful and very efficient travel consultant Eugene Phua, from Flight Centre in Northwest NSW. After my marriage to Evelyn, we got the travel bug and at least once a year we would use the services of our good and reliable friend Eugene. Nothing was too difficult for her, and she always treated us with respect and a great knowledge of her experience.

From Hyderabad we drove to Bangalore, which was a wonderful experience. After settling into our hotel, the Ramada, we had made friends with the rickshaw man Afroz who took us all around Bangalore to all the shopping centres and shops to purchase saris and other clothing. Even the tailors on hand did their fittings and repairs for a relatively small amount of money. We had him have it all shipped to us back in Australia, including a silk carpet, which came after our return to Australia without any hassle.

Today in 2021 I keep in touch with Afroz via WhatsApp and without fail, when he attends the mosque on Fridays, he always sends me a voice message, praying for our family's welfare and health. From Bangalore we flew to Madras (Chennai) and after a couple of days flew back to Singapore for a week and then home. We found by using Singapore as a base we were able to visit many places, like Vietnam, Thailand, Bali and we even visited Sri Lanka after the massive tsunami that created devastation in Japan, Malaysia and across the Bay of Bengal to Sri Lanka and south India. I just checked Google and it confirmed it was in 2011.

CHAPTER 21

The travel bug after marriage to Evelyn 1990-2019

- Singapore, Malaysia - September 1990 – October 1990
- Samoa – 29 October – 06 November 2005 with our bowling group
- Our Oriana cruise from Sydney to Singapore 25 February 2006 – 20 March 2006 with our bowling group (Ted, Marie, Malcolm and Ros)
- Tasmania 04-13 May 2007 - Japan and China May and June 2007 (Tom, Geeta, Anand, we celebrated a surprise 50th birthday for Anand's mum)
- New Zealand on Dawn Princess, 05-18 February 2008 Vietnam 2008 Hawaii 05-12 November 2008
- Hong Kong, Macau and Taiwan May-June 2009
- Egypt Israel 27 October – 04 November 2010, Israel 04-20 November 2010, USA, Florida, Caribbean cruise, Las Vegas, San Francisco, Hawaii
- Thailand 26-28 October 2012, 19 India, Chennai, 21-23 October 2012, Goa, Bangalore, Mumbai, Kolkata, Kalimpong-India 17-21 November 1912
- Thailand 18-28 January 2013 with Danny, Vivian, Edward and Jeba, it was ironic that we were destined to visit the Thai Death March on Australia Day 2013

- May-June 2019, 28-day cruise from Durbin-South Africa, Reunion Island, Mauritius, Akaba - Jordon, Suez Canal, Katakola- Greece, Kota – Montenegro, Venice – Italy
- September-October 2019 – Sydney – Hawaii USA, Seattle (3 nights), the Space Needle, Boeing Factory, flight to Vancouver Canada (4 nights), the Rocky Mountains, back to Seattle -USA to catch our cruise "The Sky Princess" P&O cruise (7 nights) to Alaska (Ketchikan) and the inside passage Vancouver Island – Canada and finally back to Seattle – USA, (1 night) then flying to Hawaii USA (3 nights), before returning to Sydney.

That was the last holiday anyone would be having for a long time as the coronavirus had hit the world and was declared a pandemic, and caused a lot of illness, death, financial hardship and worldwide instability owing to the unknown nature of this deadly virus as it reared its ugly head throughout the world, without distinction of country, colour, class or status in life.

CHAPTER 22

2019-2021 the coronavirus strikes the world COVID-19 pandemic

Thank God for His provision, we returned back from our Alaska trip to Australia and little did we know that we would not be able to travel for the last 18 months and into the near future. The whole world has been engulfed by the pandemic, and to this date it has created so much uncertainty, death, financial, personal hardship, and severe shortages with the race to find and vaccinate as many people as possible around the globe.

Thanks to Wikipedia, I was able to briefly touch on the timeline of this coronavirus disease 2019 (COVID-19), which is caused by severe acute respiratory syndrome coronavirus 2 (SARS-CoV-2). It began to circulate in Wuhan in China in late December 2019. The world had not experienced anything like this before, apart from AIDS, Ebola, SARS, and MERS, which were the new viruses of the 21st century. No vaccine had been developed for any of the above medical epidemics.

This was something new and had the scientists heading off to China to try and get to the source of SARS-Cov-2 genome sequencing, as a window on the epidemic. On 12 January 2020, the Chinese government formally shared the genomic sequence with the World Health Organization, and said the spread was under control. The very next day 13 January, Thailand reported a patient infected by novel coronavirus, it was a woman and the first known case outside of Wuhan in Hubei Province.

The CDC (Centre for Disease Control) and WHO now knew that the disease appeared to transmit easily, based on the growing number of patients. It was now called COVID-19, and the very first US patient was now confirmed, a woman who had arrived in the USA, after traveling home to Chicago's O'Hare International Airport, still feeling fine, but who after a few days would call a doctor complaining of difficulty in breathing and be admitted to a local hospital. In a short while doctors realized that she had also infected her husband.

The next day 15 January, a 35-year-old man from Washington USA arrived in Seattle-Tacoma International Airport from China after a business trip just outside Wuhan. He would become the second confirmed case in the USA.

The Chinese Lunar New Year on 24 January 2020 began the travel of over 500 million people for the New Year celebrations as is customary for people to travel to be with families at this time for almost 10 days, as the whole nation and Chinese around the world celebrate the Lunar New Year.

On 30 January 2020 the WHO declared a public health emergency, and on the 11 March 2020 declared a pandemic. Since 2021, variants of the disease have emerged or become dominant in many countries, with Delta, Alpha, and Beta variants being the most virulent. As of 20 August 2021, more than 210 million cases and more than 4.4 million deaths have been confirmed, making it one of the deadliest pandemics in history.

During the last lockdown in Sydney, Australia in 2020, I began producing and sewing reusable, washable, 2–3-layer cloth masks. I had never used a sewing machine in my life but was able to raise much needed funds for my old school and another orphanage in India and funds for MSF (Doctors Without Borders). This lockdown also gave me the opportunity to plan and publish my own book.

As there is so much suffering and despair now, I felt that God had spoken to me, and through His grace and blessings in my life, has given me this opportunity to fulfil my dream of sharing my story in the hope that it would help someone else. These are difficult times, but there is still a "Ray of Sunshine", even on a cloudy day, and there is a light at the end of the tunnel.

I sincerely hope that you have enjoyed this journey of my life, and I thank you for your support and inspiration. I hope that one day my grandchildren would be able to share this experience with their heads held high. I thank God for the gift of their lives, knowing that anyone can put their minds to doing something good, even with limited ability, but with sheer guts and determination anything is possible.

I will sign off now and wish one and all a safe, happy, healthy and a truly wonderful life ahead. God bless and stay safe. We will all come out of this COVID-19 pandemic together stronger and better for the experience we have all suffered. We take this time now, to think of the countless people all over the world who are and have been affected by this pandemic, and may we reach out to them and all those less fortunate than us and make this a better world in 2022 and beyond. Roger and out. "Ray of Sunshine"

Ray's 65th birthday-2010.

Son Graydon and daughter Ingrid special memories April 2004.

Graydon, Dad and Ingrid New Year 2019.

Brother Errol and Raymond Errol's birthday 10.10.2020.

Graydon, Valerie and 3 grandchildren Xavier, Cooper and Lily 2020.

DGH OGB – Jarvie Hall Family 2010.

Brother Don and Raymond.

Magic moments 2021.

RAAF SGT R.A. Cooke in full mess dress.

Daughter Ingrid, and my 6 grandchildren first time ever -22.09.2021

www.ingramcontent.com/pod-product-compliance
Lightning Source LLC
Chambersburg PA
CBHW070258010526
44107CB00056B/2498